MYTHS OF THE AFTERLIFE

Excellent! Annamaria Hemingway illustrates how the wisdom from ancient myths of many world cultures and religious traditions carried down through the ages offers us a sacred opportunity to unravel the mystery of life and death. This book offers a priceless understanding of why we are all immortal beings.

Josie Varga, Author of *Visits From Heaven and Visits to Heaven*

Both ancient and shamanic cultures understood that to live fully we must be initiated into the mystery of death. In Myths of the Afterlife: Images of an Eternal Reality, *Annamaria Hemingway guides us through many of the world's sacred documents that relate the experience of this basic mystery: death is not an end but an opening into another dimension of life. Equally important are Hemingway's accounts of the rediscovery of this truth in our own time through deathbed visions, near-death experiences, and our increasing awareness of the reality of mystic consciousness. This informative study will inspire readers to explore their own assumptions about the meaning of death-and life.*

Betty J. Kovaks, Ph.D., Author of *The Miracle of Death*

From birth, we are accompanied by both Thanatos and Eros, and we long to reconcile the meaning of life and death. Mythology is one method to awaken our consciousness of another world, in order to give meaning to our existence. In this excellent work, Annamaria Hemingway takes us on a tour de force through the history and meaning of the mythology of an afterlife, and she demonstrates how through myth, we can begin to understand the mystery of life and death. This is a fascinating book and I highly recommend it to any student of consciousness and those interested in what follows after death of the physical body.

Dr. John L. Turner, Author of *Medicine, Miracles and Manifestations*

Myths of The Afterlife

Images of an Eternal Reality

Myths of The Afterlife

Images of an Eternal Reality

Annamaria Hemingway

BOOKS

Winchester, UK
Washington, USA

First published by O-Books, 2011
O-Books is an imprint of John Hunt Publishing Ltd., Laurel House, Station Approach,
Alresford, Hants, SO24 9JH, UK
office1@o-books.net
www.o-books.com

For distributor details and how to order please visit the 'Ordering' section on our website.

Text copyright: Annamaria Hemingway 2010

ISBN: 978 1 84694 425 3

A CIP catalogue record for this book is available from the British Library.

Design: Tom Davies

Printed in the UK by CPI Antony Rowe
Printed in the USA by Offset Paperback Mfrs, Inc

We operate a distinctive and ethical publishing philosophy in all
areas of our business, from our global network of authors to
production and worldwide distribution.

CONTENTS

Die happily and look forward to taking up a new and better form.
Like the sun, only when you set in the west can you rise in the east

Jelaluddin Rumi

For my father, John

Chapter One

Myth: Fact or Fiction?

The term *mythology* refers to a body or collection of myths from any given tradition and derives from the Greek *muthos*, meaning tale or story, and *logos*, which is translated to mean speech. For many people, *myths* conjure up vague recollections of fanciful stories or epic tales and legends that are often associated with the fantasies of childhood fairy tales or the supernatural adventures of heroes, like Jason and the Argonauts or Odysseus, which originated in early Greek civilization. However, at a deeper level, many of these ancient stories preserve a history of how human beings have struggled to come to terms with death.

Although the most widely recognized mythologies tend to be those of the Greeks, Romans, and Egyptians, all world cultures have an important mythological heritage, such as that of the Mesopotamian, the Norse of ancient Scandinavia, the Celt of early western and central Europe, the Indian or Vedic, and that of the Christian-Judaeo tradition. While there is no specific universal myth, studies in mythology have uncovered how widespread are the many symbols and motifs that recur throughout various societies and eras. Many cultures include creation myths that tell of how the world came into being; these range from illustrating how supreme deities fashioned the Earth out of abstract chaos and myths that tell of recurring destruction and creation that are allegories to seasonal death and rebirth. The notion of a "golden age" from which the human being fell from grace is another common theme in the Christian-Judaeo tradition. The motif of the "flood" is also universal and plays a key role in myths that tell of the annihilation and recreation of the world, or a particular society. Nature myths also describe the

1

origins of the elements and the gods who governed them. They demonstrate how ancient cultures discovered and revered a sacred power and "magic" in the natural world around them and how they believed that death related to the cycles of the sun, the moon, and the tides. The relationship between the living and the dead is a common characteristic in the mythologies of many world religions.

Creation myths narrate a time of "beginnings" when, through the power of supernatural beings, a certain kind of reality was born. These stories were retold to describe a sacred history and revealed a secret esoteric *knowledge*: and through accompanying rituals, early people had genuine religious experiences in which the supernatural origins of human beings were made known, and so life assumed a far deeper sense of purpose and meaning.

Myths have often been interpreted by historians to mean false or made up stories or fables. For archaic societies, however, these narratives were valued as true accounts and were precious, because their contents were deemed to be not only sacred and significant, but also exemplary. In these early civilizations, *myths* had a very definite function. With the lack of any scientific knowledge of the workings of the universe and the projection of unconscious contents onto the outer world, complicated pantheons of gods, including the Hellenic and Egyptian deities, were created in order to establish a sense of unity with the rhythms of the natural world and provide a sacred container for understanding the mystery of life and death. These revered stories were closely linked to religious beliefs and frequently endorsed by rulers and priests. For the particular culture in which certain myths evolved, they were regarded as true narra-tives from a distant past—a primordial age when the world was still evolving. Myths provided a means to explain how the world had come into being and how various customs and taboos had been established.

Many diverse societies from those of the Mediterranean to the

Near East, Asia, and India, all include mythologies that were first passed on in an oral format and later enriched and preserved in the written word by writers and poets. The *Homeric Hymns* comprise of a work of epic poetry that records the long span of the development of Greek mythology. The Hymns are credited to the Greek writer and poet, Homer, but they continued to be revised over hundreds of years. One of the oldest of these compositions is the *Hymn to Demeter*, composed around 650 BCE that recounts the myth of Demeter and Persephone. Another early Greek poet, Hesiod, authored the epic poem *Theogony* that told of the mythical origins of the world and the gods. Anonymous bards also preserved the rich heritage of the Hindu tradition and mythology in the epic Sanskrit poem known as the *Mahabharata*, which was composed between 200 BC and AD 200 and is the longest poem recorded in world literature. These poetic epics all contained the history of figures, places, or events from the distant past and illustrated how early societies constructed their sense of time and history.

Mythology provided the foundation for many literary works from the time of Aeschylus, the early playwright, who was hailed to have been the father of Greek tragedy. He believed that his dramatic works were inspired by a vision of the god, Dionysos, and his plays are among the oldest surviving in Western literature. In more recent times, ancient myths have continued to provide a source of inspiration for many poets, including Milton, Shelley, and Keats. Writers and poets, such as James Joyce, D. H. Lawrence, and T. S. Eliot, also imagined new myths using the old sources and implementing more modern symbolism.

Myths also offered guidance through establishing models for human behavior and they provided an assurance that whatever challenges people faced, these difficulties had already been met and overcome by the heroes of mythological adventures. The characters from myths were considered to be *divine* beings and so were worthy role models that served to expand the human being's creative imagination to limitless possibilities. Myths opened a portal of communication between the profane and the sacred, an open dialogue with divine deities and mythical ancestors, and their transcendent values. They provided *living* and tangible examples through the poetic, yet powerful language of analogies and symbolism that often related to the natural world.

For example, through contemplating the continual symbolic lunar phases, the ancient Sumerians likened their own destinies and possibilities for survival to the cycles of nature. Through the world of the mythic imagination, human beings were given the opportunity to transcend the barriers of everyday consciousness and reenter mythical time that never changed, which enabled a return to sacred origins and experiencing the divine. Although myths did not guarantee moral behavior, they did provide a sacrosanct history and provided exemplary codes of conduct, which played a huge role in the evolution of consciousness. Mircea Eliade, who extensively researched the understanding and purpose of myth and ritual, writes:

> Myths are the most general and effective means of awakening and maintaining consciousness of another world, a beyond, whether it be the divine world or the world of the Ancestors. This "other world" represents a superhuman, "transcendent" plane, the plane of *absolute realities*. It is the experience of the sacred—that is, an encounter with a transhuman reality— which gives birth to the idea that something *really exists*, that hence there are absolute values capable of guiding man and giving meaning to human existence.
> (*Myth and Reality* 139)

Although it is impossible to strictly define *myths*, certain core components describe how they attempt to convey spiritual values. William G. Doty refers to the topics that frequently appear in such a debate in, *Mythography: The Study of Myths and Rituals*, which include: "subject matter having to do with the gods, an 'other world' making universals concrete or intelligible, explicating beliefs, collective experiences, or values, 'spiritual' or 'psychic' expression" (29).

In early cultures, the retelling of myths took place in *sacred* primordial time and they were communicated by priests or elders. These stories told of the beginnings of life and the world, but they also explained how mythical events resulted in the origins of death and so provided an explanation of *why* we are mortal.

Myths of death also conveyed the possibility for resurrection and renewal in the belief of a return to the primordial and divine source in a spiritual rebirth and new form of existence. Death is often referred to as "sleep" or eternal "rest." In Greek mythology, sleep and death were inextricably linked through the twin brothers, Hypnos and Thanatos. For the ancient Greeks and Gnostics, there existed the concept that human beings slept through life in a state of forgetfulness and ignorance to their true nature, which resulted in "death." An *awakening* constituted of a remembrance of the true identity of the soul and its otherworldly origins. The myth of the Mesopotamian hero, Gilgamesh, illustrates how deprivation of sleep was an initiatory practice in order to gain immortality. Gilgamesh fails to stay awake for the allotted seven days and six nights and fails in his quest. In this story, and in many similar myths, lies the imagining that death can be overcome by "waking up" to be fully present in the spiritual dimension.

Studies into the origins and definitions of myth have taken place throughout the eras. Early Greek philosophers and scholars explained myths as being allegorical and they believed that the deeper spiritual and moral meaning of these stories could be discovered in poetic images. Some viewed myths as a reconciling force between the human being and nature. Myths formed the foundation and heart of ancient Greek civilization. The early writer and mythographer, Euhemerus, compiled the body of Greek myths during the fourth-century BCE and believed them to be based on actual historical events that were then expanded and elaborated through the retelling of the stories. He suggested that the gods came into being from legends about human beings. Plato considered myths to originate from the art of language, which included that of the poets. Although he believed the poets should be closely monitored by the state, he too used a mythical mode of expression when his discourses that were based on logic and reason required emotional amplification. Varro (116-27 BCE) was a Roman scholar and writer, who established a mythical theology and viewed the poets that preserved a mythological history, as presenting an approach to the divine.

During the seventeenth-century, Giambattista Vico (1668-1744), who was an Italian philosopher and historian, suggested that myths originated from primordial thought patterns. He believed that mythology, language, and cultural traditions provided tools for investigating history. His work was largely ignored, but was rediscovered and highly regarded by later theorists. During the latter part of the nineteenth-century, academic research into myths was undertaken by scholars including Sir James Frazer, Sir Edward Burnett Tylor, and Andrew Lang, who mainly viewed mythology as representing an archaic and outdated mode of thought that was superseded by modern science. However, twentieth-century theorists rejected the notion that there was an opposition between myths and science. Sigmund Freud had a great fascination for mythology and thought mythic motifs arose from the same source of those in dreams. He was particularly drawn to the archetypal symbolism of the myth of Oedipus, from which he formulated his famous theory of the *Oedipus complex* that centered on unconscious impulses and emotions stemming from early relationships a child had with its parents. He was also influenced by the myth of *Amor and Psyche*. Perhaps this was because Psyche descended to the underworld and crossed the barriers of consciousness, a journey which Freud attempted psychologically that resulted in transformation.

Carl Gustav Jung was fascinated by the parallels found in the fantasies of his patients with severe psychotic disorders at the Burgholzil Hospital in Zurich and how they related to mythic patterns. In his private practice, Jung began to analyze his patient's dreams, which also presented images that corresponded to those found in ancient myths. As a result, he suggested the existence of a "collective" unconscious that contained primordial patterns of human behavior and experience. To begin with, Jung described the tendencies to form images from these recurring patterns as being *primordial* images, but he later named them as *archetypes* that brought into consciousness an unknown *psychic* existence that emerged from a distant past. These *archetypal energies*, according to Jung, contained the inherited experiences of humanity, which could be actualized and take "form" and thus be perceived as living realities in conscious awareness. These universal archetypes expressed themselves in the similarities between the myths of different cultures.

Mircea Eliade contended that myths ritually reenacted a return to the source of primordial creation and that the rejection of the mythological world resulted in the loss of the sacred, which gave rise to many human anxieties. Joseph Campbell believed that the retelling of myths and the world of the mythic imagination could provide insights about individual psychology. Claude Levi-Strauss concurred that myths reflected patterns in the psyche, but he viewed these models to be fixed mental configurations that encompassed pairs of opposites rather than unconscious feelings or urges.

Within all these varying definitions of myth, a concise short definition would be the following, as outlined in the Columbia encyclopedia:

> A myth, however, is generally a story that takes place in an imagined, remote, timeless past and tells of the origins of humans, animals, and the supernatural.

Chapter Two

Archetypes and Symbols

The mythological world comprises of a universal language of metaphors and symbols, which when translated, can provide a sacred container for understanding the mystery of life and death. Although human beings can readily discuss topics perceived through the five senses, death is outside the realm of conscious experience and, therefore, difficult to articulate through language alone. In order to enrich our myths about dying, we need to be able to interpret the fluid yet archetypal patterns and symbolism reflected in ancient myths, which are then seen to echo sacred teachings stored in the collective unconscious.

Giving a clear definition of the term *archetype* is a difficult task; for archetypal content is expressed through the use of metaphors, and so always contains a hidden context that defies all rational explanation. Archetypes can only be identified through the effects they manifest, and their origins remain unclear. However, they refer to a set of images that have been indelibly stamped on the psyche of the human being since time immemorial; an example would be the alternating darkness of night and the light of day.

Human beings have continually sought to determine an explanation for the world in which they live. The pre-Socratic philosopher Heraclitus (535-475 BCE) renounced his kingdom in order to seek wisdom and knowledge. The great body of his work was lost. However, fragments survive that illustrate how his thinking was not only philosophical, but also poetic and prophetic. He believed that the core essence of matter was *energy* and *wisdom* and he likened the cosmos to an alchemical eternal fire in which all things were in a constant cycle of regeneration.

Aristotle sought to determine philosophical answers from a more theoretical standpoint, and he concluded that insights could be gained through expanding the powers of perception. Pythagoras viewed mathematical reason and logic as providing a language that explained the prophetic cosmic principles of the universe, and he coined the world *philosopher* to mean the lover of wisdom.

The famous Platonic dialogues can be viewed as expanding the theories of Socrates, who was said to have instilled Plato (428-348 BCE), with a quest for enlightenment. Although Plato's discussions appear as lively conversations between wealthy young Athenians, at a deeper level, they seek to answer questions that may reveal the mysteries of the soul. He developed the concept of *forms*, in which qualities such as beauty have an eternal essence or energy. Plato's discourse on *forms* suggests primordial *forgotten* knowledge and so represents an early understanding of unconscious contents.

It is evident to see that there is a relationship between Plato's theory of *forms* and the archetypes. The archetypes were to give an experiential foundation to Plato's theory, for both related to the idea of an image that was formed, but exists outside of everyday consciousness. However, the *forms* were imagined to be absolute, transcendent, and eternal. The archetypes differ in that they are not static inherited memories, but rather alive and fluid, and their dynamic force reflects the changing images of life that can dissolve and then, out of the old, be created anew.

The world *archetype* comes from *arche* that means "primal root" or "origin," and *type*, which is translated as "image" or a "copy." Archetypes can thus be viewed as imprints of recurring primordial tracings and patterns, which are stored in the collective unconscious of human beings. The archetype can also integrate all possibilities from the past and the future and, like the mythical Janus head—it looks both forwards and backwards.

The idea that the human psyche contained material that was

unavailable in conscious awareness was speculated upon for thousands of years by a great many Greek philosophers, including Dionysius and Plotinus. The mystical traditions of India recorded in the Holy Scriptures of the *Vedanta*, also pursued such thought, as did mystics from the Middle Ages, including Meister Eckhart and Boehme. By the late nineteenth-century, debates on the unconscious realms were of paramount speculation and popularity. This vast storehouse of the psychic history of human beings was thought to be "neutral" in that there was no differentiation between good and bad, or beauty and ugliness. However, these contents revealed themselves through a confrontation with consciousness.

The archetypes have a transpersonal, invisible quality that nevertheless manifests as a structured reality. Myths with a religious orientation can help people to rediscover the concept of an eternal and transpersonal dimension through reconnecting with the archetypal images found in ancient myths. Cultural heritage from around the world contains myths that depict the archetypal image of "light," which symbolizes a numinous or sacred encounter. Archetypes retain this numinous value and are still vitally important in the psyche, because they influence the behavior and attitudes of the human being. When archetypes appear, they can often herald changes taking place within the individual, who is searching to discover a more personal, meaningful myth. These archetypal energies continue to be experienced in the world of dream images that we all encounter every night.

Jung's work with the unconscious and the archetypes led him to experience many archetypal images of death and rebirth. In *Memories, Dreams, Reflections*, he describes a stunning archetypal vision depicting the ancient solar myth of death and renewal (179). He also narrates an instance where he felt his soul fly away from him to the "land of the dead," which he believed to be a paramount experience, because it signified the soul forming a relationship with the unconscious (191).

Jung was convinced of the reality of the collective unconscious and the archetypes. He encountered many archetypes and the ones he felt to be central were: the *persona*, the *shadow*, the *anima/animus*, the *Self*, the *wise old man*, and the *mother*. He believed these images had universal value; for unlike temporary human existence, the archetypes are timeless and emanate from the realms of the unconscious, and these energies continue to appear in the consciousness of individuals and act as spiritual guides.

Archetypal energies that often manifest in ancient myths of death and resurrection and stories of otherworldly journeys are those of the *shadow* and the *Self*. The dark shadow aspect of the persona embodies all the negative traits of the personality that can often be transferred to another person. In some cases, the shadow can take over the complete personality of the individual, who is unaware of these negative qualities.

In ancient Western traditions and throughout Eastern mythology, the opposites contained in the archetypes remained united. However, over time a division took place. This is particularly noted in the Jewish deity, Yahweh, who contained both light and dark aspects, but following Christian reformation became an all encompassing "good" god, as the negative attributes were passed over to the devil. However, Eastern traditions incorporated intellectual intuition and, therefore, the gods and goddesses remained *whole*. The Hindu goddess, Kali, who represents time and change, manifests both light and dark aspects. Known as the Madonna in Western cultures, the goddess no longer contains her shadow aspects, but the darkness still exists and cannot be denied and so was projected onto the psyche of the human being. A life review or judgment of the soul following death is commonly found in the mythologies of world religions, such as the deceased being ushered into the presence of the Egyptian god, Osiris, or the Day of Judgment associated with

Christianity.

The archetype of the *Self* is referred to as signifying wholeness and contains symbolism depicting unity, such as the *world navel* or the *axis of the universe*, and represents a union of opposites that makes order out of chaos. It also constitutes a merging of the personal and transpersonal, and so signifies a numinous encounter between the human being and "God." Icons of religious figures, including Christ and the saints, are often adorned with a halo or circle of light, and thus provide an outer symbolic manifestation of the holy or numinous. The Bible describes the rewards to the individual for gaining wisdom, which is likened to shining like the stars for eternity: "Those who are wise shall shine like the brightness of the sky, and those who lead many to righteousness, like the stars forever and ever" (Daniel 12:3). Iconography denoting the numinous quality of a deity are also preserved and illustrated in the depictions of halos surrounding the Hindu god, Krishna; the Greek god, Apollo; and the Buddha. The climax of the ancient Isis Mystery rites, celebrated in ancient Egypt, also culminated in deification when an initiate became identified with the sun god, was anointed, and received the crown of life. The motif of the circle or *mandala* is also featured in ancient and modern-day burial rituals as offerings of flowers, which are often formed as mandalas and so make them a fitting symbol of the Self. The placement of flowers on the graves of the deceased not only symbolizes our feelings of empathy, but also an unconscious hope for resurrection.

The relationship between the ego and the Self is of paramount importance and reflects the individual's relationship to the concept of a creator, which is often symbolized in religious myths. Throughout history, humans have possessed an intuitive awareness that an inner center exists, and the Greeks referred to it as being the internal *daimon*. The Egyptians thought it manifested as the *Ba-soul*, and the Romans paid homage to the *genius* found within each individual.

The belief in a higher power providing guidance in life is contained in the archetype of the Self, which is structured around *a priori* knowledge of "God" or deity representing a primordial unconscious sense of perfection and unity. The human sense of nostalgia over personal and cultural origins is believed to stem from the stirrings within the psyche of this original knowledge. During the initial stages of life, before the birth of the ego, the Self forms the primordial totality of the psyche and is symbolized in the circular image of the tail-eating serpent, known as the *uroboros*, which can be traced back to early Egyptian, African, Mexican, and Indian mythologies. The serpent provides an image of self-sufficiency; for through digesting its tail, self-fertilization takes place. Childhood is spent separating from the Self and forming the ego's development. The latter period of life is when the ego and Self reunite, encompassing the totality of the conscious and unconscious, in a process that Jung named as being that of *individuation*. The alternating cycles of union and separation between the ego and the Self occur continually throughout the life span of the human being, and this individuation process is associated with immortality, as personified in the ancient Egyptian myth of Osiris.

Symbols

The modern-day human being often finds symbolic forms that express archetypal energy unfamiliar and hard to translate. However, they are still vitally important in the psychic life of the individual, who still needs to be aware of these symbolic messages that not only provide an outer objective meaning, but also awaken human consciousness to a hidden profound interpretation.

The world *symbol* has its origins in the Greek *symbolon* that is formed from *sym*, translated to mean "together," and *bolon*, which refers to "something thrown." For the early Greeks, symbols represented the two halves of a coin or object that signified a pledge, and they were later used to prove the identity of the holder. The concept of something missing that is then restored can psychologically be interpreted to mean retrieving the missing part of the individual, in order to create a totality or sense of wholeness.

Symbols appear to facilitate the transformation of psychic energy, which means that the symbol is *alive* and can convey meaning to an unknown unconscious content. Jung writes, "A symbol really lives only when it is the best and highest expression for something divined but not yet known to the observer. It then compels his unconscious participation and has a life-giving and life-enhancing effect" (*CW* 6, 476). In order for a symbol to have such an effect, it adopts a form and produces a pattern that creates an expanded state of awareness, but the instinct of the individual must recognize a prevailing pattern within the image. *Energy* and *form* are the central components of the symbol and what is separated by an objective state of consciousness is united through a profound symbolic consciousness, which is not within the grasp of rationality. Understanding symbolic representation requires bypassing the intellect and opening to the mystery that the symbol may reveal. To be considered a *living* symbol, an intense emotional response to the image must take place, as a symbol is constantly evolving, and energy is in perpetual motion. This theory applies to all symbolism, including that of religious origin. In *Living Myth: Personal Meaning as a Way of Life,* D. Stephenson Bond writes:

> The symbol of the cross. A chalice. An altar. A mosque. The Star of David. A prayer wheel. A Tibetan mandala. A totem pole. A crystal you want to buy in the New Age Store. Does it have intensity? Does it stir the imagination from sleep? Does it grip your fascination? If so, then it is living. If not, then it has died. If so, then it has become symbolic. If not, then it has become simply historical. (82)

The energy and form that constitute symbolic imagery reveal the nature of the archetypes as being patterns of psychic energy. Continuing importance of revelations and messages from the archetypal realms was, according to Jung, due to the self-absorption of the contemporary individual, which resulted in a meaningless existence. He believed that the way to rediscover a deeper meaning to life was to be found through studying myths, legends, fairy tales, poetry, and visual images. By interpreting and comparing the parallels found in the analogies of ancient myths, Jung theorized that the capacity to form symbols, which were expressed by the ancients in their rituals and rites, still resided within the collective unconscious of contemporary human beings.

The hermeneutics or interpretation of mythology involves collecting universal myths and giving the archetypal images and symbolism a voice. In this way, it is possible to understand and interpret the parallels that reinforce primordial motifs.

Chapter Three

Resurrection Myths

Fascination with the *mysterium tremendum* surrounding death and a possible afterlife state has been recorded since time immemorial. From birth, humans face the paradox of walking with the shadow of Thanatos, representing death, and Eros, symbolizing life, as constant companions. There is little contemporary education on how to hold the tension of these diametrically opposing instincts, and prepare for transition from earthly existence. However, for many ancient societies, arrays of resurrection myths contained recurrent archetypal patterns; they described mythological figures and descents to the underworld, ascents to the celestial realms, and encounters with heavenly or dark deities. These myths that were closely associated with decay and regeneration in the natural world reflected the belief and hope that death is always followed by rebirth.

Ancient resurrection myths that seek to shed light on the mystery of death have been a constant source of curiosity. Humans know that death is inevitable, which has resulted in a collective quest to continually seek out imaginative ways to explain how life and death are inextricably linked. For the ancients, these stories provided a basis for understanding a deeper meaning of existence, because the insights and wisdom were gleaned through sacred encounters with mythological ancestors or Divine Beings. The wealth of resurrection myths recorded throughout history is vast, but in the following examples, the motif of death, rebirth, and spiritual enlightenment is a recurrent one.

The Myth of Gilgamesh

Although the epic of *Gilgamesh* is not a resurrection myth in the strictest sense, the story provides a valuable foundation through illustrating how human preoccupation with anxiety over death and a mission to discover immortality has resided in the collective unconscious.

It was from the ancient world of Mesopotamia, where Gilgamesh reigned as historical king of Uruk, in the region between the Euphrates and the Tigris around 2750 BCE that the text originated. All reference to the epic vanished for over two thousand years, but in 1850, parts of the clay tablets that bore the story were discovered and later translated. This geographical area heralded the dawning of Western civilization, and despite scientific and medical advancements of modern-day cultures, the myth is still a source of inspiration into penetrating the deeper layers of fascination and fear surrounding death.

Gilgamesh is described as being two parts divine and one part human. However, in spite of his divine qualities, Gilgamesh is a tyrant and servant of his ego. He has a mirror image in his companion, Enkidu, who, although more human than divine, retains more of a sense of connection to the natural world. The pair journey into the forest and slay the monster, Humbaba, for Gilgamesh believes that if he wishes to live eternally, this will only be achieved by attracting fame while living his earthly life. After killing the creature, Enkidu has two prophetic dreams related to dying in which images of a gloomy Mesopotamian afterlife are revealed. In one dream, Enkidu sees his death and journey to the land of the dead, where he is transformed into a bird by a bird-man figure, who accompanies him to the under-world.

In ancient Mesopotamia, the deceased were envisioned as taking the form of a bird and their mythology conceptualized the idea of a "bird-soul." From the reference made in the dream to an afterlife state, it would appear that this early culture did not believe that death marked the end of consciousness. Instead, they thought that death implied the body separating from the spirit and, although the body was buried in the earth, the soul or spirit moved on to a different realm. The epic of Gilgamesh, like all myths, mirrored gradual advances in consciousness and may well have provided the foundation for the concept and development of an immortal soul, which later became referenced in the New Testament. The letter of Paul to the Romans states that "to those who by patiently doing good seek for glory and honor and immortality, he will give eternal life" (Romans 2. 5-7).

Following the dreams, Enkidu then falls ill and does eventually die, leaving Gilgamesh distraught with grief and in fear of his own mortality. The death of Enkidu symbolizes the death of the pure part of Gilgamesh that must be reborn in order for him to achieve a union of opposites, and realize his *eternal* Self. He has an ancestor, Utnapishtim, who has been granted eternal life, and sets out to find him. Like the characters from similar *hero* myths, Gilgamesh encounters many trials on this journey to seek immortality. The images he encounters, while running through a dark tunnel to eventually reemerge into the light on his way to find Utnapishtim, are motifs of death and spiritual rebirth and are experienced in myths of otherworldly journeys, including contemporary near-death experiences. However, Gilgamesh is not yet conscious enough to experience such a transformation.

Gilgamesh finally locates Utnapishtim, who advises him that he must stay awake for seven days and six nights in order to discover the secret of immortality. The number seven symbolizes wholeness and is found throughout world mythologies, such as the seven heavens described by Dante in *The Divine Comedy*. This sacred number is also referenced in the Old Testament when Elisha sneezes seven times and a child comes back to life (2 Kings 4:35). Gilgamesh is so tired that he immediately falls asleep and fails in his quest, but he is then told of a plant that provides a cure for the fear of death. He takes the plant and places it on the ground, but a passing innocent snake takes it. The snake symbolizes rebirth in nature and is a universal motif of regeneration depicted in many ancient myths. In the nocturnal journey of the Egyptian sun god, it is the serpent that gives birth to the newly born sun. The innocent serpent simply eats the plant to renew itself through shedding a skin. The motif of the snake still manifests in the dreaming state of contemporary human beings, symbolizing the healing and regenerative abilities that arise from the unconscious.

Gilgamesh has a violent past and is a self-destructive individual lost in his ego. He loses his gifts and is unable to succeed in discovering the secret of eternal life. However, he does eventually find redemption and undergoes a spiritual rebirth on his journey home. His inner quest perhaps has been to explore and integrate the humanness of his divinity that encompasses physical death, in order to realize his divine Self from human existence. He subsequently returns to his city transformed and continues to rule, but as a more benevolent leader, who shares the wisdom of his mythic journey with his people. The historical epic of *Gilgamesh* depicts the inner journey that is necessary to come to terms with the anxiety surrounding death through symbolizing the struggle to integrate a union of opposites—life and death. The story also hints at a sacred marriage of earthly humanity and eternal divinity that is preserved in the myth, which reflects the deeper levels of meaning of all mythological traditions.

The Myth of Inanna

The myth of "The Descent of Inanna" was first recorded in about 1750 BCE, and Inanna was said to be a moon goddess. She was often referred to as "Queen of Heaven" and was loved and revered throughout ancient Sumeria. In the myth, Inanna is queen of the celestial realms and the Earth, but she has no knowledge of the underworld and the part of her own identity that is concealed within its darkness in the form of her sister, Ereshkigal, queen of the underworld. However, Inanna hears the desolate cries of her sister and, in order to achieve true wisdom and understanding, she must descend from the Great Above to the Great Below. This journey of descent into the darkness of death, followed by rebirth and ascension back into the light, will enable Inanna to experience a spiritual rebirth through an encounter with Ereshikigal—a reflection of Inanna's other Self. These central motifs of personification and transfiguration continue to appear in the mythological teachings of many world religions.

In order to enter the realms of the underworld, Inanna must be prepared to abandon her power and adornments; this sacrifice and willingness to face death to experience rebirth is the common denominator in the many myths of resurrection gods and goddesses. Through her descent, Inanna will gain necessary wisdom on both life and death. She gathers the seven *me* or attributes that define her royal status and makes her way to the gate of the underworld, known as the Land of No Return. As she passes through each of the seven gates, she is forced to relinquish her clothing and accessories denoting her royal power, for these outer elements are worthless in the realms of the underworld. Inanna enters the throne room of her miserable sister and is confronted by the seven judges of the netherworld, who glimpse her hidden split-off character and sentence her to death.

Ereshkigal's existence is bleak in the underworld and she symbolizes the archetype of the "wicked witch," who is filled with anger, rage, and rejection. Inanna's death, however, causes her pain ands she moans in agony as her sister dies, for Inanna represents the discarded light part of her Self that also wishes to be reborn, and thus enable her to become complete. The dark goddess receives comfort through the compassionate mirroring of her discomfort from small creatures that the God of Wisdom has sent to save Inanna. Such kindness has a transformative effect and opens Ereshkigal's heart to a more generous state, and she eventually agrees to release her sister. The tiny creatures then sprinkle the food and water of life on the rotting corpse. As with the heroes and heroines in similar myths symbolizing resurrection—the goddess is reborn.

Inanna prepares to leave the underworld, for she has transcended death, and her rebirth creates a passageway between the conscious in the Great Above and the unconscious in the Great Below. This portal must now remain open, but nobody has ever been allowed to leave before. New conditions must be set and Inanna is told that she must provide a substitute to take her place. She offers her husband, Damuzi, in exchange for her freedom, and it is eventually agreed that he will divide his time in the underworld and spend six months of the year with Inanna, who thus grants him both death and everlasting life. Through this loving gesture, Inanna alters cosmic order and promises renewal.

Damuzi portrays the image of the mythological shepherd king, who through death becomes immortal, and he is often described as being a representation of the future image of Christ. He is also depicted as a vegetation god that dies following the long hot summers, and then comes back to life in the spring to renew the seasons and the crops. The rites and rituals that took place annually in Sumeria to commemorate Inanna and Damuzi acknowledged and reenacted the duality of life merging into death, and death heralding new life.

The story of Inanna, recorded thousands of years ago, has continued to be a source of fascination, because it contains a universal message of hope for resurrection. Inanna made a descent to the underworld from which there was thought to be no return. She died and then achieved the seemingly impossible—she experienced rebirth. She also opened the portal between the Great Above and the Great Below, and this channel of communication must remain open. Efforts to maintain dialogue between the conscious and unconscious realms has continued to be the quest of human beings.

The Myth of Osiris

The ancient myth of the dismemberment and rebirth of Osiris originated in Egypt over three thousand years ago and was recorded by the Greek writer, Plutarch of Chaeronea. Osiris was pharaoh of Egypt and renowned for civilizing the country. However, he was lured by his brother, Seth, to enter a lead-lined chest, which Seth then cast into the river. After overcoming many trials, Isis, the wife of Osiris, managed to locate all the body parts of her dead husband, except for the phallus, which she recreated. For the ancients, the phallus symbolized the thrust upwards towards the spirit realms and may possibly also represent the *axis mundi*, which connects the earthly realms to the divine transpersonal realms of existence. Isis, known as the Great Mother that held the secret of immortality, refashioned her husband's dead body and through a magic ritual brought him back to life. Osiris then ruled the underworld as Lord of the Dead. Dismemberment and eventual assimilation of the divided parts symbolized Osiris as being an immortal vegetation deity, who incorporated the rites of death and rebirth. For these ancient people, the corpse of the deceased symbolized something mysterious that was part of the resurrection process.

Ancient Egyptian agricultural societies were governed by the rhythms of the natural world, such as the annual flooding of the Nile or the rising and setting of the sun each day. For the Egyptians, the dismemberment and resurrection of Osiris in a transformed body, revealed an archetypal model to understand the mystery of death and what may lie beyond. Osiris was described as being barley or wheat, and all the deceased were referred to in the same manner. He was also known as the Lord of Decay and the Lord of the Abundant Green, symbolizing the corruption of the physical body and reunification of the deceased with Osiris at death. Through referring to the mythical historical resurrection of the god — the unknown was explained and the similar fate of all humans was revealed, and became a sacred reality.

For the ancient Egyptians, it was a portion of the soul that was believed to separate from the body at death, in order to follow the journey of the sun god Osiris/Ra. The rituals of bringing Osiris back to life were commemorated and reproduced as closely as possible by the Egyptians, and concluded with a pole or pillar representing the eternal life force, being placed upright and symbolizing transcendence over death. Complex funerary customs and rites were observed faithfully in order to ensure reinstatement of the deceased, who was identified with Osiris, into the eternal cycle of life. The ancient Egyptians believed in the god's supernatural abilities as a resurrection deity that they would unite with following death.

A life review or judgment is also associated with Osiris, as the deceased were ushered into his presence in the Hall of the Two Truths on the first stage of the mythic eternal journey. At one end of the hall, Osiris was seated with forty-two divine Egyptian gods, who acted as judges. A set of scales held the heart of the deceased on one side and a feather representing truth on the other. Each time a negative act was recorded, the scales were checked to see if they balanced. If they did not, the deceased would be eaten by the goddess, Ammut, who manifested in the form of a crocodile and a lion. However, when the scales were evenly balanced, the deceased would be rewarded and pass on to the next phase of gaining an eternal and pleasant afterlife.

The life review, followed by a coming into the light, symbolized how leading a just earthly existence would result in everlasting life and becoming "one" with Osiris. This concept of merging with the Divine was later expanded in Christian mythology and led to the idea that all human beings have an immortal soul and would be reunited with God following death.

The myth of Osiris was not just associated with the moment of death, but rather enabled the initiates to lose their fear of dying and so discover a new sense of morality that transformed their ways of being in the world.

Resurrection is the central archetypal motif in the myths of dying and reborn gods, which symbolizes the germ of life existing in a possible afterlife state.

Chapter Four

The Books of the Dead

The sacred texts, known as The Books of the Dead, offered hope to humanity through detailing the mythic journey the deceased embarked upon to an afterlife state.

The Egyptian Book of the Dead

The Egyptian Book of the Dead was known as the Pert em hru, which was translated to mean "a coming forth into the light," and originated from the spoils of Egyptian robbers, who ransacked the tombs and found papyrus scrolls containing funerary texts belonging to the deceased, alongside their mummified remains. These texts affirmed an unshakable belief in the myth of everlasting life. A preserved papyrus in the British museum states:

"Thy soul liveth, she rejuvenatheth herself, she knoweth in eternity, for ever. She goeth to the place where Osiris is; she goeth and cometh upon the earth for ever."

The funerary texts comprise of a vast collection of magical spells, prayers, litanies, hymns, and mythological reenactments originating from many different dynasties, over a five thousand year period. Many of these early pyramid texts date back to 2350-2175 BCE. They were carved on tombs and temple walls and acted as transition guides that protected and provided a safe passage, through the use of magic spells, for the deceased pharaohs on their journeys to the afterlife. A central component of the texts was the judgment of the deceased in the presence of Osiris.

However, around 1700 BCE, these practices that were previously designated to royalty began to be used more commonly throughout the general population, with the advent of coffin texts that could be engraved on the coffin of the deceased or appeared in scroll form. During the long span of the funerary texts, many changes evolved throughout Egypt and were incorporated into the book, thus making it far more complex. The sun god, Ra, featured in later traditions, but in more ancient texts, Osiris was deemed Lord of the Underworld.

The followers of Ra believed the deceased would accompany the sun god and other divine deities in a solar barque on their symbolic nocturnal journey through the land of the dead. They would pass through Tuat, which was a miserable realm full of terrifying monsters and challenges to overcome. After overcoming these trials, the sun god would return newly born to the sky at dawn and it was believed that the deceased, after completing the sacred voyage with Ra, would be similarly revitalized and gain insight into the secret of eternal life. The *Amduat* that describes the mythological twelve hour passage through the night world not only provided guidance for the deceased, but also for the living, as the Egyptians remained convinced that life on earth was a preparation for the eternal journey following death.

In the earlier traditions, the followers of Osiris believed him to be Lord of the Underworld in a realm that was everlasting, and thought they would join him in a blissful paradise known as the "Field of Rushes." A papyrus from *The Egyptian Book of the Dead* depicts the Field as being one of eternal harmonious life and fertility, conjuring up an image of a paradisiacal Nile Valley state. Spells associated with transition to the field describe how the entrance to the afterlife state is located on the eastern horizon, where the sun rises. The deceased traveled to the Field by boat and had to answer questions from the ferryman before gaining admission. Arriving at the Field, the deceased would enjoy a bountiful and harmonious eternal existence.

The value of the vast body of funerary texts not only preserved ancient Egyptian myths symbolizing death and the possible afterlife of the immortal soul, but also provided a legacy for the validation of Jung's theory of a collective unconscious, through the many images added and revealed in the Pyramid texts of the New Kingdom, which displayed great similarities to those of the dream world and the unconscious.

The Tibetan Book of the Dead

The mythic teachings of *The Tibetan Book of the Dead*, also known as the *Bardo Thodol*, originated from the oral traditions of ancient Tibetan cultures, prior to the advent of Buddhism, and were first recorded in the written world during the eighth-century AD, by the grand master, Padmasambhava, who introduced Buddhism into Tibet. Although little is known of the pre-Buddhist practices, one of the main characteristics of these early religions seems to have been a preoccupation with death, and what may exist beyond. Rituals for the dead included sacrifice and food offerings, which were made to ensure safe transition for the deceased into an envisaged afterlife.

Padmasambhava later buried the texts of *The Tibetan Book of the Dead* in central Tibet, in an area known as the Gampo Hills, and transmitted the power for their rediscovery to his dharma heirs. They were later unearthed by Karma-Lingpa, who was a direct descendent of one of these chief devotees. The *Bardo Thodol* is essentially a guidebook that seeks to ensure liberation for the deceased and the dying and comprises of a set of instructions on how to navigate the intermediary *bardo* (translated to mean gap) state between death and rebirth, with the aid of an enlightened teacher. This liberation is achieved through a set of directives for the six forms of liberation.

The symbolic teachings contained in the *Bardo Thodol* are specifically aimed at liberating the deceased from the confusion and sense of duality that arises from identification with the perceived ego sense of the meaning of existence. In a hazardous journey through the intermediary *bardo* stages between death and rebirth that involves encounters with both divine and dark deities, the deceased experiences the illusion of death and recognizes the impermanence of all things. The ensuing dissolution of the former false projections of Self can result in a transcendent state of enlightenment and illumination, in which a merging with the Light of Pure Reality or Dharmakaya takes place. Although this sacred text is primarily focused on the dying and the deceased, there is also a valuable message for the living—for the bardo states of death and becoming are fully present in everyday life, as humans struggle with uncertainty to discover their deeper identity and find the essential qualities of the Buddhist teachings, which are love, wisdom, and compassion.

The Maya Book of the Dead

The ancient civilization of the Maya people had a rich cultural history. However, many of their ancient manuscripts, known as codices, which recorded their way of life, were destroyed by Spanish invaders. In Maya mythology, the funerary art that was discovered on coffins, precious stones, and ceramic vases, symbolized their belief in life after death. At the moment of death, the Maya thought that the soul would leave the body and enter the underworld, known as Xibalba. The challenges of this journey through the underworld were known, and precautions for a safe transition were made through the funeral art depicted on the coffin and offerings to accompany the deceased. On this journey through the underworld, images of which were richly preserved on the vases, the soul would encounter archetypal entities that included the Hallucinatory Serpent, The Great Bearded Dragon, and the Serpent of the Bloodletting. After successfully navigating this dangerous terrain, the soul would be reborn in glorious resurrection. Much of this journey of rebirth was based on an important section of the *Popul Vuh*, a historical epic of the Quiche Maya that recorded the oral mythological stories of the Maya people, and was written by an anonymous Guatemalan Indian, sometime after the Spanish conquest.

The epic tells of the victory of the Hero Twins, who entered the underworld to avenge their father's death. After overcoming the deities of the underworld through trials of death and rebirth, which included dying into the flames of a huge fire and being reborn five days later, they then subsequently hacked themselves to pieces in a rite of dismemberment and returned to life. Appearing rejuvenated, they eventually gained immortality and ascended into the heavens where they were transformed and entered the eternal realms of the sun and the moon. Excavation at ancient Maya archeological sites provided relics of ancient funerary vases that represented codices, which, when placed in consecutive order, represented the equivalent of *The Maya Book of the Dead.*

The ancient Maya civilization had a great interest in myths of an afterlife following physical death. It would appear that they imagined that the harshness of their earthly lives was reenacted during the trials that their souls encountered in the underworld, before being reborn and entering the heavenly realms. The miraculous death and resurrection of the Hero Twins mythologically symbolized their belief in a celestial ascension and rebirth.

Of great importance to the cult of the dead in ancient Maya history was also the link to the cycles of vegetation. The archetypal imagery of plant life represented an unknown psychic aspect in the mystery of death and rebirth, which symbolized the alchemical transformation of vegetation regenerating from dead matter and the elements of water, earth, light, and air. For these early people, who saw that the body decomposed in a similar manner, vegetation imagery and metaphors provided hope for similar rebirth.

Ars Moriendi: The Christian Book of the Dead

The Christian Book of the Dead comprises of a vast body of texts compiled in medieval Europe during the Middle Ages that reflect the Christian myth of death. The subject was of great interest to Europeans living in this era, as scenes of mass burials, and the burning of corpses and execution of supposed witches and heretics were part of daily life. Through constant exposure to death, coupled with the collapse and corruption of the establishment, religious scholars of the day were prompted to compile such a collection of texts.

As with The Books of the Dead from other cultures, the symbolic message in the *Ars Moriendi* was not just for the terminally sick or those close to death, but also addressed how the individual could cope with the impermanence of life. Coming to terms and preparing for death was revealed in the literature of the first part of the work, which instructed the living on how to understand death through symbolism, metaphors, and parables. These analogies were often based on rich and famous dignitaries of the church and state and illustrated the folly of seeking a successful existence through accruing material possessions, which in the face of death were worthless. Instead, the texts symbolized that wisdom was gained through the realization that death was the master of life and that one should be constantly vigilant to ensure life was lived in accordance with Divine principles, which would prepare the individual to face death, whenever it may appear. The second part of the texts dealt with the experience of dying and aiding people who were in the process of transition. Monks from the Franciscan and Dominican orders compiled a manual to instruct priests on how to support the dying and prepare them for the mythic transcendent journey of the soul following physical death.

The myth of an afterlife was a central theme of the *Ars Moriendi*: and preparation for making a good death, through living a worthy life, enabled the soul of the deceased to enjoy eternal bliss. Christianity is founded on the core myth that human beings transition from earthly life. Easter celebrates the death and glorious resurrection of Christ, who told his followers that in order to have eternal life, it was necessary to undergo a spiritual rebirth of water and spirit and be "born from above" (John 3:7).

The Books of the Dead portrayed death as a threshold to a new cycle of existence in the myth of a return to the eternal light. They all reiterated a similar theme—that of using the symbolism of death as a motivating force to live life consciously and well.

Chapter Five

The Ancient Mystery Cults

For ancient Greek and Egyptian civilizations, myths preserved a divine legacy and provided rituals of communication with their gods. Through yearly festivals, comprising of secret rites and initiations commemorating the eternal return of the deities, these early people reactualized the narration of original primordial events, and so entered the realms of sacred time. This repetition of mythological symbolism instilled hope that the eternal life of the gods provided a divine model allowing human beings to determine their place in the cosmos.

Dionysos and the Bacchanalia

The personality of Dionysos included the absorption of the characteristics of two non-Hellenic deities: A god from Thrace, who was associated with the vine, altered states of ecstasy, and orgy, and Zagreus, who was known as a Cretan mystery god, and deemed to be one with Osiris, Egyptian Lord of the Underworld and god of immortality. Dionysos was a nature god associated with fertility. He experienced a "second" birth, following dismemberment, and this renewal symbolized wholeness and the theme of initiation into the rites of death and rebirth. He is further associated with death and resurrection through descending to the underworld and bringing Semele back from the dead. However, he paid a high penalty to achieve the release of his mother and enter the underworld of Hades— his masculinity—symbolized by a phallus, formed from fig-wood that he instituted as a symbol of the cult. Having entered and returned from the underworld, Dionysos was believed to communicate with the dead. The ancient cult and religion of

Dionysos celebrated life and the eternal source from which that life emanated.

In the Dionysian Mystery rites, the image of the god conjured up an altered state of consciousness, which was induced in initiates by drinking fortified wine mixed with plant or herb derivatives that contained hallucinogenic properties. This prime stimulant enabled ancient people to experience states of mystic consciousness through lifting them out of the limitations of the "sober" self. The rites that formed part of the Dionysian religion were based on finding the "god" within. The myth of Dionysos was not just an analogy depicting life and death through the symbolic decay and regeneration of a vegetation deity. Instead, it was a living myth in which the continual death and rebirth of the god was experienced as a reality by the initiates. These participants were mainly female, for the world of Dionysos was the world of the feminine. The primal wildness and abandonment these women displayed symbolized the inner essence of the god, who churned up the diametric opposites of the ecstasy of life that was surrounded by the turmoil of death.

Dionysos was represented during the rituals by a large mask depicting his penetrating energy of confrontation. Invoking communion with Dionysos was accomplished by partaking of the wine mixture and the intoxication, trance-like state, and orgasmic sexual activity resulted in accessing an altered state of consciousness, whereby the shackles of conformity and the ego were abandoned. The mask was lifted on all that was civilized within individuals and they were plunged into an intense frenzy, in which the exuberance of life was fuelled by death, and the past, present, and future all existed in the moment. In this feral state, perception was altered and participants were initiated into the mysterious secrets of nature and felt the presence of Dionysos within themselves. He existed in the flesh of the wild beasts they consumed, in the wine they drank, and in the effigies of the phallus that they displayed—no duality existed—and life and death subsisted simultaneously in every moment. Through the repeated reenactments of such rituals, both men and women could continually imagine a merging with Dionysos, and lived their lives interwoven with that of the god; and through the projection of the god, the paradox of life revealed itself.

The myth of Dionysos celebrated the continual process of death and rebirth. Jung explained rebirth as an archetype that repeated one of the primordial affirmations existing in many different cultures, throughout human history. He believed that these affirmations manifest psychically in rituals that transcend everyday life and reveal the continual cycle of life through renewal and transformation (*Jung on Death and Immortality* 39).

Dionysos personified the divine archetype of the raw and indestructible forces of the natural world, and through these rituals that invoked altered states of consciousness, the disciples of the god manifested the same qualities within themselves. In the ensuing orgies of dismemberment of sacrificial animals and ecstatic sexual orgies, the followers of Dionysos affirmed the eternal cycle of death and rebirth.

The Orphic Cult

Orpheus was said to the son of the muse Calliope, and the Thracian river god, Oeagros, although some accounts refer to him as being the offspring of both Oeagros and Apollo. He is best known for his journey to the underworld to rescue his wife, Eurydice. He fails in this quest by disobeying the gods, and his famous backward glance toward the realm of the dead may symbolize his attempts to unravel the mystery of death. Through his descent and return from Hades, initiated by the soothing melodies of his lyre, Orpheus was considered to be an intermediary between the living and the dead.

Orpheus symbolized the hope of transcending death through the magical quality of his music and words. In one part of the sonnets to Orpheus, the great poet, Rilke, suggests the divine power of the music of Orpheus even soothed the rocks the Maenads stoned him with. The decapitated head of Orpheus was still heard to be singing as it floated down the river Hebrus, signifying that after death, he still existed in some form. The Greek philosopher, Plato, described Orpheus as choosing a future life of a swan in the *Republic*.

Orpheus was not recognized as a god, but it was believed that he possessed supernatural power manifesting through his music and poetry, and he was known as a seer and religious emissary. He founded a religious cult that was based on the deity of Dionysos, but was reformed. Life after death was an important feature of the Orphic Cult. Initiates believed that as Orpheus had demonstrated the power to calm those in the underworld, he could also intercede on their behalf if they lived a pure life according to his example. While initiates in Dionysian rites transcended consciousness through wild ecstatic states, the followers of Orpheus sought to access a state of profound mystical enlightenment through purification. Symbolic death and rebirth rituals were part of the Orphic initiation rites.

Orpheus was known to perform magic through his music and he was often associated with spells and incantations that facilitated altered states of consciousness amongst initiates, animals, and even the forces of nature. On the expedition of Jason and the Argonauts, he charmed the sirens, calmed a turbulent sea, and soothed the clashing rocks. A painting discovered on an ancient vase depicts a tranquil scene of people listening to his song that enabled them to depart for a while from linear time and experience a transcendent state of perception. For the Greeks, Orpheus had knowledge of the mysterious divine world of the gods, and his language contained a power that surpassed normal speech, thus entrancing and captivating those hearing his words. He conveyed otherworldly wisdom and sacred realities through stories, which provided the central theme of the cult.

Orpheus was closely aligned with nature and the religion was one founded on the sacred "mysteries" of the gods. The Orphics thought that the human being comprised of a Dionysian eternal soul incarcerated within the confines of a flesh covered Titanic body. Through living a pure and pious life, initiates believed that the soul could be freed from its last mortal incarnation and actualize its immortal destiny—achieving the status and home of the deified soul.

There is some reference to the fact that ritual sacrifice did not include animal offerings, as Orpheus taught the initiates to refrain from killing. However, ritual offerings were made, followed by prayer and sacred chanting. Part of the rites also included stepping in and out of a circle or enclosure that symbolized the wheel of life and then climbing a ladder, a motif that served to bridge the earth to the heavens. The Orphic rites of initiation and the history of Orpheus were recorded on small gold bars that were buried with the dead; and several of the inscriptions detailed instructions for the deceased upon their arrival in Hades. The initiates were reminded that they must drink from the Lake of Memory, rather than the Spring of Forgetfulness. Having drunk from the lake, the soul is rewarded for a pious earthly life and, along with other joyful initiates, enjoyed an eternal harmonious and pleasant afterlife state.

The Eleusinian Mysteries

The myth of Demeter and Persephone is primarily a vegetation myth. Persephone's descent and return from the underworld resulted in her being associated with the seasons. The time spent with Hades represented the fall and winter, when the earth would remain fallow and barren. Her return symbolized spring, regeneration, and renewal of the crops. Her mother, Demeter, revealed the sacred mysteries of the corn and both mother and daughter were personified in the symbolism of the corn. The old crops, represented by Demeter, gave way to new growth embodied in the figure of Persephone.

Persephone was also one of the few mythological figures that visited the realm of the dead and was allowed to leave, thus symbolizing transformation and renewal. This central motif of death and rebirth was, therefore, not just confined to the crops, but was also an allegory for the destiny of human beings. The rites and rituals of worship to the two goddesses also prepared the initiates for death and immortality; for it is believed that the rites consisted of a ritual using a dead looking barley stalk. This metaphor of the grain symbolizing immortality was also repeated by St. Paul. When speaking of how the dead came back to life, he states, "What you sow does not come to life unless it dies. And as for what you sow, you do not sow the body that is to be, but a bare seed perhaps of wheat or some other grain" (1 Corinthians 15: 36-37).

The significant religious aspect of the Mysteries was that the initiates believed an encounter between the queen of the under-world and the living would take place in the rites that were shrouded in secrecy, but continued to be celebrated for over a thousand years during the Greek month of Boedromion, which would fall around September/October.

The initiates would purify themselves by bathing in the sea and sacrificing a young pig to Demeter and Persephone. The pig symbolized the Great Mother, and was also an emblem of other-worldly projection. Initiation at Eleusis comprised of two levels. The first involved eating small cakes and drinking the *kykeon* in a holy communion. The second stage of initiation involved the candidate preparing for as long as a year, in order to be part of the Grand Mysteries, which concluded with a sexual union between the High Priest and Priestess.

A prerequisite for initiation required the participants to enter an altered state of consciousness and become passive and receptive to experiencing psychic visions and apparitions, which shed new light on the darkness of death. This altered state of consciousness appeared to expand the imagination into a state of extrasensory perception, giving rise to sacred imagery. In order to facilitate such an altered state, participants would prepare by fasting and undergoing intense spiritual practice. It is an accepted fact that hunger can induce hallucinatory states. However, this altered state may have been intensified through drinking the *kykeon*, which was said to contain roasted barley groats mixed with water that fermented into alcohol, but may well have also contained a third ingredient of a mind-altering hallucinogenic substance. Research into ancient vases that were unearthed indicates that the barley was infected by a fungus or mushroom that was contaminated with ergot, which in the late 1930s was discovered by the Swiss chemist, Albert Hoffman, to contain similar chemical alkaloids to LSD. Fungal fermentation produced the bread from Demeter and the wine from Dionysos and also enabled ancient cultures to triumph over death through the use of the mushroom properties.

Initiates of the rites were not required to learn theoretical knowledge, but experience a direct epiphany. Even though exactly what took place in the Mysteries has remained a closely guarded secret, evidence gathered from ancient writers, such as Homer and Pausanias, (together with depictions on ancient funerary vases), strongly suggests that initiates experienced revelations and spiritual awakening through communing directly with higher realms of consciousness, personified by the figure of the mother goddess, Demeter, and the goddess of rebirth, Persephone.

The Mysteries of Osiris

The mystical initiations of ancient Egypt were widely documented by Greek writers, including Plutarch. He described how these rites took place in the dark underground chambers of the sacred temples and symbolized a journey to the netherworld and the reenactment of the resurrection of Osiris.

During the period of the Middle Kingdom, the religion of

Osiris was the major one in ancient Egypt. Public rituals of bringing the god back to life were commemorated annually at the end of November and took place in Abydos, the site of Osiris's tomb. Pilgrims flocked to the sacred sites as a reenactment of the journey of the god setting sail in his barge took place. Prayers and chanting for the resurrection of the god followed, as a chest symbolizing Osiris was placed to rest at his tomb. A three day period of mourning gave way to jubilation and a celebration of the deity's resurrection. For the participants, this was a festival in which miracles and epiphanies occurred, and their descriptions of the culmination of the festival were translated to mean the appearance of "god." These annual rituals and rites continued for thousands of years into late Roman times.

The central theme of the Mysteries was that eternal *life* came from *death*.

Chapter Six

Alchemy and Immortality

The roots of alchemy can be traced back to ancient Babylonia, Greece, Arabia, Egypt, China, and India. Gradually, the texts spread to Europe during the Middle Ages and later, Latin alchemical texts came into existence.

Ancient Egypt was imbued with alchemical concepts and was referred to as "The Land of Khem," which was translated as "black earth." The word *alchemy* was thought to have originated from *khem* or *chemia* meaning "black," and the origins of this ancient art were bound to death and immortality. Alchemical texts, originating in Egypt, describe transformation of dead matter (the body) into the rebirth of the soul and were associated with early Egyptian burial rituals and rites, and the myth of Osiris. Alchemy may also have formed the core of early religious experience in ancient Egyptian mythology. In *Anatomy of the Psyche*, Edward Edinger writes:

> The earliest forms of religious expression—which indicate the first separation of the ego from the archetypal psyche—seem to be associated with burial rites. The outstanding example of death as the genesis of religion and consciousness is the elaborate mortuary symbolism of ancient Egypt. This is also clearly, the origin of alchemy. The embalming of the dead king transformed him into Osiris, an eternal, incorruptible body. This is the prototype of the alchemical *Opus*, which attempts to create the incorruptible Philosopher's Stone. (168)

According to the myth, the sealed chest that contained the bodily parts of Osiris was covered with black lead before being thrown into the sea. Osiris asphyxiated in a coffin sealed with lead, and this represented the death of *prima materia*—or the physical body. The lead that lined the coffin was associated with causing madness, and the early writings of Olympiodorus of Thebes, a historical writer from the fifth-century, suggest that this hostile environment acted as a uniting element, which reconciled all aspects of the god.

The lead coffin represented the grave of Osiris, in which the god mysteriously prepares for rebirth, but this resurrection also symbolizes the renewal of the world. The apparent death-like state is only a temporary disappearance of consciousness, for Osiris is immortal and within the divine god, the form of the divine spirit is assumed in death. What was of supreme importance to the alchemists was that bodily remains contained the possibility for the transformation of matter and new life.

Alchemists viewed the bodies of the deceased as symbolizing buried treasure and so they believed that the perfect human being was a corpse, because the infinite nature of the individual was buried within the body, resembling the mummy buried in the tomb. Early Egyptian art depicts the resurrected Osiris in the form of a ladder. This image symbolizes the pure spirit freed from the corrupted earthly body climbing the ladder to the heavenly realms. Symbolism representing eternity was also thought to originate from early Egypt where the deceased were believed to be transformed into stars surrounding the sun.

Psychologically, alchemical funerary symbolism represents an experience of psychic reality, for the psyche cannot manifest as a detached entity until the demise of the physical body. The mythic realms of the collective unconscious resemble the underworld, and descent into this terrain is referred to as a *nekyia*, because a meeting with the autonomous or independent psyche is felt as a death of this world

Resurrection following death and burial is also associated with the alchemical beliefs in the regenerative cycles of the natural world, and with the germination and planting of seeds. Ancient Egyptian art work depicts sprouting stalks of grain emerging from the deceased body of Osiris, and this symbolism represents the emergence of an eternal Self that arises from decay, and so ancient Egyptian alchemy represented a reconciliation of opposites that became unified at the moment of death.

During medieval times, many of the alchemists were also physicians engaged in the rituals of preparing a cadaver for the afterlife. They not only recorded their work in ancient texts, but also illustrated the symbolic analogy in surreal art forms. An example of this type of work is Holbein's *The Dance of Death*, painted in 1538, which depicts a man contemplating a skull. The skull is evocative of human mortality and alchemical change. Edward Edinger writes, "To reflect on death can lead one to view life under the aspect of eternity, and thus the black death head can turn to gold" (*Anatomy of the Psyche* 168).

In much of the art work illustrating death from this period, the forces of good and evil are seen to collide, thus generating archetypal images including the devil and angelic beings dueling for the soul of the dying individual. This struggle of opposites proved to be an illusion; for in reality, beneath the conflict, was to be found the complete Self in the reconciliation of these opposites. The belief that the moment of death symbolizes such a conflict appears to have an archetypal quality. In ancient Rome, fighting duels between gladiators were held in commemoration of the dead and may have represented this dualistic clash between good and evil.

For the alchemists, discovering the secret of matter was a search for God and was thought to be found in the philosopher's stone. However, some alchemists from the Middle Ages realized that this quest for the stone symbolized something that could only be discovered within the psyche of the human being. The alchemical stone (the *lapis*) represented an unidentified phenomenon that was eternal and could not be dissolved or misplaced, and was likened to experiencing a mystical vision of God within the soul of the individual.

During the Renaissance, many alchemists viewed the metaphor of the transformation of lead into gold as symbolizing the emergence of divinity within the human being. In psychological terms, the base matter in alchemy corresponded to the immaturity of the ego that would be transformed into divine essence by the philosopher's stone. This process would result in changing the corruptible body into an eternal body of light. *Remembering* that a divine essence existed within humans represented the underlying goal of the alchemists—a quest in which, through corruption and decay, the imagination would be stimulated to recognize these divine origins.

The invisible figure of Hermes was connected to alchemy and he was known as a guide between life and death, who embodied the archetype of the unconscious. He was associated with the metal mercury that possessed the ability to remain fluid in temperatures that make other metals hard. Described as a *psychopomp* or leader of the soul, Hermes Mercurius was of great importance in medieval alchemy and personified transformation, because it was he who accompanied and directed the opus or central aim of the alchemists and guided the initiates through the various stages of the process. Seeking a deeper meaning, portrayed through alchemical metaphors, involved hearing both the voice of the philosopher, and the stone, embodied by Hermes.

Although alchemical theories are often confused and chaotic, it is the archetypal symbolism contained in the texts that relates to chemical change and transformation that is of prime importance. In the alchemical Latin writings of the Middle Ages, the procedures of reducing solid matter through chemical means to a pure state were associated with the myth of death heralding new life, and these alchemical experiments mimicked the processes of the natural world.

One of the principal themes of the alchemical opus was that of redemption and the release of the divine soul incarcerated in matter. This metaphor of retrieving the concealed "god" from matter was underscored by the ancient Gnostics in the myth of Sophia, who personified divine wisdom. During creation, she descended into matter and then lost her way and became captive to matter, and so became the hidden "God" that is in search of freedom and salvation. The transcendent nature of alchemy alters perception and changes a lead-based everyday consciousness into a golden understanding. Everything is reflected in its pure archetypal form, which is eternal and encompassed within the Divine, and this realization enables a universal redemption. The most essential teaching of the opus was that through symbolic metaphor, it provided the human being with a goal to attain this divine liberation, and this was apparent to the ancient alchemists and philosophers.

While reading through ancient alchemical texts, Jung found them to be provocative and stimulating and he came to the realization that the alchemists wrote in the language of symbols. One night while immersed in this world, he had an archetypal dream and found himself in the seventeenth-century. He interpreted the dream to mean that he needed to study alchemy in depth, and gradually solve its principal meaning. The decade that Jung spent reading through old texts led him to compare alchemy, and its Gnostic roots, to his work in the unconscious realms. In summing up the important dimensions that alchemy provided, he writes, "When I poured over these old texts everything fell into place: the fantasy images, the empirical material I had gathered in my practice, and the conclusions I had drawn from it (*Memories, Dreams Reflections* 205).

The origins of alchemy were bound to death and immortality.

Chapter Seven

Otherworldly Journeys

Many mythic traditions include stories of heroes, prophets, kings, and everyday mortals, who enter the threshold of death to learn its secrets and bring back messages for the living. But why does the human being look to images of the dead, imagined realms of an afterlife, and the stories of those on the threshold of death? Perhaps it is because only the myths of the dead can illuminate the darkness of death. In *The Dominion of the Dead*, Robert Pogue Harrison writes:

> The primary reason why the dead have an afterlife in so many human cultures is because it falls upon them—the dead—to come to the rescue and provide counsel when that debilitating darkness falls. Why this special authority? Because the dead possess a nocturnal vision that the living cannot acquire. The light in which we carry on our secular lives blinds us to certain insights. Some truths are glimpsed only in the dark. That is why in moments of extreme need one must turn to those who can see through the gloom. (158-59)

The Myth of Er

In book V11 of the *Republic*, Plato provides a discourse on what he believes to be the deeper reality of human existence and refers to an ascendant journey as providing true wisdom. He then amplifies the philosophical value of such a symbolic journey of ascension and relates the story of a return from death. In this narrative, a warrior named Er, who is said to be the son of Armenius of Pamphylia, is killed on the battle-field. However, when the dead are collected ten days later, Er's body shows no sign of decomposition even though it displays no vital signs of life. His lifeless body is returned to his family and arrangements for a funeral were made. Two days later, he had been laid out on the funeral pyre and, much to the astonishment of his comrades, Er comes back to life. He subsequently relates a near-death journey that includes a description of consciousness leaving the physical body, encountering archetypal divinities, and witnessing Divine Light. Plato writes:

> He said that, after his soul had left him, it traveled together with many others until they came to a marvelous place, where there were two adjacent openings in the earth, and opposite and above them two others in the heavens, and between them judges sat. These having rendered their judgment, ordered the just to go upwards into the heavens . . . and the unjust to travel downward . . . with signs of all their deeds on their backs. When Er himself came forward, they told him that he was to be a messenger to human beings about the things that were there, and that he was to listen and look at everything in the place. (X: 614 b, c, d)

Er then recounts how the souls reaped rewards for just behavior in life and punishment for ill deeds. Plato has probably drawn on similar analogies from ancient myths of the Egyptians or Zoroastrians that include the concept of judgment following death to promote moral behavior in earthly life.

Er is then taken on a journey with other souls. After the fourth day, they arrive at a place where they can look down to a huge column of light that shines over the entire earth and heaven. This light resembles a rainbow, but it is brighter and purer. The following day, they reach the light and see it stretching from heaven and holding everything in the universe in place. The light resembling a rainbow is a symbol of the portal that links the heavens to the earth and binds the entire cosmos together, which is held in place by the Spindle of Necessity and the goddesses, Clotho, Lachesis, and Atropos, who govern fate and destiny. Lots were cast to determine future destinies and were scattered between the souls for a further life on earth. The souls were then required to drink water from the River of Forgetfulness, in order to have no lasting memory of what had transpired, and then return to life in the form of a shooting star. However, Er was forbidden to drink and was to remember all that he had witnessed.

Er's ascent to the heavenly realms contains a similar sequence and much of the same symbolism found in otherworldly journeys spanning over thousands of years. Although the symbolic and archetypal content of such experiences are interpreted according to cultural mythologies and beliefs—the message imparted from such a journey always remains constant, and seeks to convey an expanded awareness of the human being's place in the cosmos. Plato's mythological account of a near-death journey provided a metaphor for gaining philosophical wisdom. He believed this knowledge could be obtained by taking care of the immortal soul while on earth through virtuous behavior, and thus prepare for death and the journey beyond.

The Near-Death Journey recorded by the Venerable Bede

One of the earliest written narratives of a near-death journey was recorded by the Venerable Bede, an English monk and eighth-century historian. In *The History of the English Church and People*, Bede describes how a man, Drycthelm, who lived a seemingly devout life, became seriously ill one night and died. The following morning, he came back to life and described what he had witnessed, as he entered the threshold of death.

Drycthelm narrates how he was met by a good looking man, dressed in a luminous robe, who guided him through the various stages of the afterlife. The first appears as a vision of hell, which is full of tormented souls. Then, as his guide vanished, Drycthelm was left in the dark with hideous spirits that threatened to seize him. However, a bright light came towards him and the evil entities vanished. He then realized that the light was the guide in the shining robe. Drycthelm then entered the clear light that formed a meadow full of spring flowers, but he was told that this was not the Kingdom of Heaven. Finally, Drycthelm is led to a more beautiful place suffused in an even brighter light that made the meadow pale in comparison. He hopes to enter this paradise, but his guide suddenly turns around and takes him back along the road they had just traveled. Drycthelm is then told that he has witnessed the fate of the soul following death comprising of: hell for those who have committed evil deeds, a pleasant place for those who must await the final Judgment Day to enter heaven, and the destiny of those that had led exemplary lives— admittance to the celestial realms and the glorious light that he had witnessed on his journey. Drycthelm is then instructed to return to his body and is advised that through living a more pious life, he too, will reap the rewards upon entry into paradise. He is reluctant to leave the beauty and light that he has witnessed.

Upon returning to his body, Drycthelm told his wife that he must lead a very different life following his experience. He then prayed at the village church, divided up all his property and became a monk, spending his time in contemplation and counseling those who wanted to live their lives in preparation for eternal life and heavenly bliss.

This early narrative of a near-death journey foreshadows the images and symbolism of the realms of hell, purgatory, and the reward of heaven for the just, which are contained in Christian mythic stories of similar otherworldly journeys from medieval times, in which the central characteristic is that of a *conversion*. Such myths portray the hero as having led a sinful life, but becoming transformed following a visit to afterlife realms.

Bede suggests the purpose of Drycthelm's near-death journey

was to instruct others and raise them from a state of spiritual dormancy, so that they may undergo a similar spiritual transformation. This account portrays a vision translated from the perspective and consciousness of an early Anglo-Saxon era. However, many similar narratives carry the same powerful teaching, even though they sometimes manifest in different images and forms that reflect the mythologies of many diverse religious traditions and cultural anomalies.

Muhammad's Nocturnal Journey

Islamic spirituality began with the revelations contained in the *Qur'an*. The Prophet Muhammad was said to have received these communications directly from God/Allah following a period of meditation in a cave at Mount Hira. In total, the Holy Scripture comprises of 114 chapters, and each one, referred to as a *surah*, gives guidance on how to live life in accordance with the will of Allah.

Muhammad was also reported to have embarked upon a nocturnal journey known as the *al-mi'raj* and ascended to the celestial realms on the back of a mythical horse. He then met with previous prophets, including Adam and Abraham and also encountered angelic entities. Traveling through the seven stages of heaven, Muhammad witnessed images of both hell and paradise and the suffering or joy of their respective residents. Muhammad is overwhelmed as he floats into a dazzling light and encounters the divine presence of Allah and he finds words alone cannot convey the ecstasy he has experienced. He is then endowed with spiritual revelations, some of which he cannot disclose. He then descends back to the earthly realms and is disappointed at having to return, but he is assured that he will experience memories of the bliss of his vision in divine worship known as the *mi'raj* of the faithful. The Ascension of the Prophet is celebrated annually on the twenty-seventh night of the month of Rajab.

Such otherworldly journeys and mystical visions have played a major part in the myths of world religions and the spiritual evolution of human beings. These visionary powers, which enable glimpses of other realms of consciousness, were more prevalent in ancient times and were viewed as positive experiences. The Buddha was said to have gained enlightenment while meditating under the Bodhi tree. The Old Testament of the Judaeo-Christian tradition includes examples of similar visionary states, such as Moses talking to Yahweh from the burning bush (Exodus 3:2), and Isaiah's vision of God (Revelations 6:1). Similarly, the New Testament details such mystical events as the temptation of Jesus in the desert (Matthew 4:1-11), and St Paul's vision on the road to Damascus (Acts 9:3-9).

Mythic journeys to an afterlife state have been imagined in a myriad of ways and reflect the constant immortal yearnings of human beings. These images and symbols describe a similar archetypal model that can be described as both a thought pattern and an emotional experience that satisfy an unconscious emotional hunger within the human psyche and reflect spiritual beliefs handed down the generations in an oral tradition.

Many diverse religious mythologies envisage an afterlife state that also provides a powerful reminder on how to live a more authentic earthly life. The ancient Egyptians believed that following death and judgment, the soul of the deceased would be reunited with the sun god Osiris/Ra. The sun changed its position in the sky throughout the day and then "died" each night and so these different stages and locations were translated as being the destinies for the soul in the afterlife. The dark underworld was linked to the night and was where the soul was judged. If this judgment received the approval of the gods, the soul would leave the underworld never to return and would come forth into the Field of Rushes where the sun rises and enjoy a blissful afterlife state. The Egyptians also thought that the soul could journey to the sun itself and so could exist in the Field and the sun at the same time. For the Egyptians, the afterlife constituted of a journey into new life that was symbolized by the dying and reborn sun and was a destiny to prepare for and look forward to.

The Aztecs believed in a paradise known as Tlalocan, which was an eternal realm of abundance and permanent summer. However, this heavenly bliss was reserved for those who perished in the storms sent by the rain god, Tlaloc, and most mortals ended up in the underworld known as Mictlan, which was ruled by the lord of the underworld, Mictlantecuhtli, and his female consort, Mictlancihuatl. Although this netherworld was considered to be one of darkness, the Aztecs also worshipped the sun, and so it could be that these ancient people believed the souls of the dead could experience the light, as the sun voyaged through Mictlan to the eastern hemisphere, where it would rise again.

For the ancient Celts, there existed the belief that the dead remained in their burial tombs with their belongings. These burial mounds were also thought to be the home of ancient Celtic gods that were banished to the underworld following Christian intervention. This underworld was considered to be a kind of *Valhalla*—a place where the souls of those killed in battle would spend eternity and continue to duel. The Isle of Avalon is famously associated with King Arthur, and although it has never been clear where it was actually located, claims were made by the monks of Glastonbury that Avalon was the old name for Glastonbury. The ancient Britons were of Celtic origin and Avalon was the place where souls would gather to commence a new life. In Celtic mythology, Avalon was a hallowed place bathed in eternal summer and joy that was abundant with flowers and fruits.

The early Greek poets, including Hesiod, wrote of a lost mythical "Golden Age" when Golden Men were created by the gods and lived a harmonious existence. They did eventually die, but this was a gentle transition and following death, they transformed into divine spirits that would watch over ordinary mortals. But this idyllic state came to an end and humans lost the possibility of experiencing a paradisiacal afterlife and, following death, they would instead be confined to the underworld. However, over time, this gloomy fate of the dead began to change in the idea that for a privileged few, a blissful afterlife would be experienced in the Elysian Fields also described as the Isles of the Blessed. The Greek writer, Pindar, who wrote in the fifth-century BCE, introduced the idea of judgment for the deceased in the underworld where the good are rewarded and the unjust are condemned. The worthy souls traveled to the Elysian Fields and chose a new earthly carnation. Following three earthly lives, each of which was judged in a similar manner, the soul was liberated to enjoy eternal paradise in the Fortunate Isles, which was very similar to descriptions of the Elysian Fields, but located in a different area. Due to the dismal outlook of an afterlife state spent in the underworld, many Greeks looked to the teachings of the Mystery Cults and the promise of an eternal paradise.

In the Hindu tradition, there is the belief that the spark or *atman* of the divine Ultimate or Absolute, known as *Brahman*, lives within every living being. Following death, the eternal *atman* or soul is judged according to good or bad *karma* that has accumulated over a lifetime. Hindu mythology is very complex and describes multiple heavens and hells. However, these abodes are not permanent resting places, because there is a constant cycle of death and rebirth, until "right action" and eliminating all desire results in a realization of "god," which can manifest in the many Hindu deities that include Vishnu, Shiva, and Krishna. The Hindu heavens are located north of the Himalayas and are paradisiacal realms where those who are awaiting their next reincarnation enjoy a stay of pleasure and luxury.

The original teachings of Buddhism promoted the belief that it was possible to become liberated from the endless cycles of death and rebirth through shedding the shackles of desire and attachment and attaining the state of *Nirvana*, which is often described as a state of bliss and results from letting go of all sense of self, but this is not death or an afterlife existence. These teachings that were primarily directives for the abstemious monks did not permit any desires, not even those for a blissful eternal hereafter. However, in Mahayana Buddhism, which originated in India in the first-century BCE and spread its way throughout Asia, a new train of thought emerged that placed less emphasis on reaching the state of *Nirvana* and focused on the concept of many pleasant rebirths in more blissful and heavenly realms. The ultimate goal was still thought to be achieving *Nirvana*, but for people who found this difficult, rebirth into a pleasurable next world made the task seem easier. The Buddha Amitabha, known as the Buddha of Measureless Light, was not of this world like the Buddha that founded Buddhism, but presided from a separate universe in the West. He had experienced countless rebirths and had been a monk in one lifetime that attained enlightenment and so had become a *Bodhisattva*, the equivalent of a Christian saint, and had created his own paradise. This Buddha promised his disciples that he would appear to them when they came close to death, so that they could approach this transition without anxiety and prepare for paradise in their next rebirth into the Land of Bliss.

In ancient Jewish myths, there exists the memory of the paradisiacal state reflected in the Garden of Eden, which was imagined to be a realm beyond that of the earth and is described in the stories of celestial ascents and visions of Enoch and Ezekiel. In other accounts, this heavenly paradise is described as being a place where the chosen souls would stay until the Day of Judgment. In the Old Testament, the dead slept in the shadowy world of Sheol, which is described as a place of dust and continual darkness and can be likened to the Greek description of Hades. It was only Yahweh and angelic beings that inhabited the celestial realms.

Dante's poetic masterpiece, *The Divine Comedy*, reflects thirteenth-century Christian mythological beliefs about the life of the soul after death. The epic contains descriptions of a journey through the realms of hell and purgatory, which results in purification and transcendence to the celestial realms and an ecstatic unification with a Divine source. Written it Italian, the work has retained a timeless quality, because through the symbolism of his mystical vision, Dante carried his audience into an understanding of mythic motifs that seek to convey a universal message.

For the Native Americans, the natural world symbolized a manifestation of the sacred. Life after death signified a reunification with the ancestors and the beginning of the individual's deeper spiritual connection to all of creation. The proverbial Garden of Eden was mirrored in the imagining of a transition to the land of the Happy Hunting Ground.

Otherworldly journeys reflect imagined visions of another reality beyond that of the sensory world, in which death and rebirth is a central theme.

Chapter Eight

The Realms of the *Imaginal* World

Throughout the evolution of human consciousness, a vast array of mythical motifs and archetypal recurring patterns reflect *imaginal* visions of another dimension beyond that of the sensory world, in which death and rebirth is a central theme. As far back as the Ice Age caves of France and Spain, the murals discovered on the cavern walls may have illustrated scenes of prehistoric visionary near-death journeys that depict an afterlife state.

The powerful motif of an "otherworldly" journey is to be found in the mythologies of many ancient civilizations and is also contained in Holy Scriptures, such as The Bible, The Books of the Dead and the Qur'an, which all make reference to an archetypal journey following death. However, is there a possible explanation for the existence of an *imaginal* realm from which such out of the ordinary perceptions arise? French scholar, Henry Corbin, who was a leading authority on the religion of Islam, put forward the theory of a *mundus imaginalis* that may answer this all important question.

The Mundus Imaginalis

The *imaginal* realm is one that enables a vision to translate symbolism, metaphor, and analogy. Resurrection myths of early cultures contained symbolic analogies and motifs of regeneration. That of Chiron also spoke of the human being as possessing both mortal and divine qualities, and the effort required to integrate both the light and dark aspects of the psyche. Chiron suffered a mortal wound that symbolized the dark shadow of his personality that feared death. To end his pain, he descended into the underworld and crossed the threshold into the realm of death. Chiron spent nine days and nights in Hades. The number nine plays an important part in world mythologies and signifies the culmination of a successful search. In Greek mythology, Demeter spent nine days wandering the earth looking for her lost daughter, Persephone. The ancient Egyptians referred to nine as representing the "Mountain of the Sun" and in many early religions, this number corresponded to the spheres of both heaven and hell. Nine also symbolized an ending and a new beginning that was associated with decay and regeneration in nature and the death and rebirth of the human being.

In the myth of Chiron, his gestation period in the underworld signified an initiation into death. As he gazed into the darkness, he thought he could see a faint glimmer of gold and he remembered that Hades, Lord of the Underworld, was also known as Pluto, who, although god of the dead, was also known as the god of riches, because precious metals and crops were said to manifest from his kingdom in the netherworld. Intervention from Zeus resulted in Chiron ascending from the underworld to live eternally in a constellation of stars. The symbolic analogy contained in this myth reflects the dynamic of regeneration, which is elusive and so difficult for human beings to grasp, but, through the wounds of life, we can sometimes expand our awareness. In *Mortally Wounded*, palliative care specialist, Dr. Michael Kearney writes, "It is as though it takes life's incurable wounds, the hurts that cannot be made better, to constellate the Chiron dynamic in our own psyches, that is, to awaken its healing power in our own lives" (150).

The myth of Chiron, like all resurrection myths, symbolizes the primordial motif of infinity. The metaphorical language of myth was distinguished, experienced, and understood by the ancient Greeks, which enabled them to differentiate between temporary and eternal life, without the need to intellectualize. For many indigenous cultures, including the Pawnee, this under-standing was also apparent and death was viewed as a transition to a portal beyond space and time. David Abram retells an old Pawnee myth in which a dead man manifests as a ghostly apparition, and says, "I am in everything; in the grass, the water" (*Spell of the Sensuous* 219). For these people, as in the narratives from many Native American mythologies, the dead are not leaving the world, but merely journeying to a land beyond the horizon where the ancestors gather.

Ancient cathedrals, mosques, and temples are central buildings in many world cultures. They act as portals that open a door into the symbolic content of a mythological treasure chest of spiritual principles and religious beliefs passed down the generations from early civilizations. Jung writes, "Their temples and their sacred writings proclaim in image and word the doctrine hallowed form of old, making it accessible to every believing heart, every sensitive vision, every furthest range of thought" (*CW* 9:1, 7).

Perception and awareness of this normally invisible dynamic, is also accessible through works of art. In *Heaven and Hell*, Aldous Huxley writes that transcendence into other realms of reality can be accessed through the primordial images of light and color, and that creative endeavors can contain archetypal symbols that have the power to *remind* us of the existence of an *imaginal* world:

> Along with the preternatural lights and colors the gems and ever-changing patterns, visitors to the mind's antipodes discover a world of sublimely beautiful landscapes, of living architectures and of heroic figures. The transporting power of many works of art is attributable to the fact that their creators have painted scenes, persons and objects which remind the beholder of what consciously or unconsciously, he knows about the Other World at the back of his mind. (119-20)

These images that remain fluid in the imagination provide an accessible gateway into an alternate realm. The domain of the *imaginal* world differentiates between individual fantasies and transpersonal experiences, because the latter are stimulated by mythic elements. Corbin provided an ontological or metaphysical explanation for the *imaginal realm* in, *Spiritual Body and Celestial Earth.* He writes that this realm is one that does not exist as an empirical or observed reality in the physical world, for if that were the case, such manifestations would be perceived by anyone. It was also evident that such realizations and perceptions could not be incorporated into the intellectual world, because they are made up of dimensions that are of no importance to the five senses, even though they retained spatial and bodily qualities. These types of phenomena could not be placed in the category of the unreal, but needed a metaphysical explanation that placed them in an intermediary world known as the *mundus imaginalis archetypus* (87). In short, Corbin suggested a classical distinction between an imagined realm, which was perceived in response to stimulus provided through the five senses, and an *imaginal* world that was real and accessed through a transcendent or higher functioning of the imagination.

Images from such a realm can complement rather than oppose logic, for archetypes possess a kind of knowledge that unveils the mystery and essential qualities of existence; becoming open to the *imaginal* enables the numinous or sacred to enter and penetrate our consciousness. Rituals and rites also facilitate entry into the realms of the *mundus imaginalis.* Participants in these events leave historical time and enter mythical primordial time, known as *illud tempus,* which is eternal and never changes. Rituals provide the opportunity to transcend from the profane to the sacred through metaphors that reveal archetypal patterns and symbolism.

The ancient rituals and rites of *Samhain,* meaning "summers end," saw a time when the structure of the ancient Celtic tribes dissolved back into primordial chaos in preparation for a new order to begin, as they celebrated the coming of the New Year on the eve of 31 October. All hearth fires were extinguished, and in the ensuing darkness, a huge bonfire was lit to represent the symbol of the waning sun that would be fortified through the fire by *magical* means. From this sacred fire, branches were lit to rekindle the hearth fires in preparation for the New Year. Samhain was also believed to be the one time of year when entities and spirits from other realms could make their presence felt. Such rituals represented an initiation into death and rebirth through the symbolism of lighting the new fire in the presence of the dead.

During the festival of Samhain, the profane met a sacred threshold. A liminal *imaginal* period existed where past, present, and future merged together and the cycles of nature, which included that of the human being, were seen to have endings and new beginnings. Ancient civilizations like the Celts were ritually structured and this gave form to human existence, not on a surface value, but at a deeper reality. Joseph Campbell writes, "A ritual is an organization of mythological symbols: and by participating in the drama of the rite one is brought directly in touch with these, not as verbal reports of historic events, either past, present, or to be, but as revelations, here and now, of what is always and forever" (*Myths to Live By* 97).

The celebration of the Day of the Dead, which still takes place throughout Mexico at the end of October, originated from the myths of early Aztec cultures that worshipped the sun; these ancient people believed that deceased souls assisted the sun's journey across the sky and then reaped the rewards of a blissful eternity. Mixed with Christian mythological beliefs of the Spanish invaders, these rites and rituals evoke the duality of life. In these festivals, the living create skeletons of the dead and make preparation for the return of departed spirits and so symbolize the continual motif of life, death, and rebirth. The living are often to be seen partying with images of the deceased in graveyards, and the afterlife state is celebrated with humor in the little clay skeletons that are visible everywhere.

Such festivals reenact ancient resurrection myths symbolizing that death can be considered an occasion for joyous festivities rather than sorrow. A similar image of death being a cause for celebration was found at the site of the Etruscan tombs. The Etruscans were an early Italian civilization and their mythological beliefs included the idea that all things manifested into existence through the divine power of their pantheon of gods, which included the absorption of Greek deities. In Rome, the Villa Giulia has a collection of Etruscan artifacts that depict how these early people believed in a heavenly afterlife state that would be experienced as an eternal feasting. Their visions of this paradisiacal realm were preserved on the walls of the underground tombs that displayed images of dancers, animals, and lute players living in a state of everlasting enjoyment. One of the most important pieces of Etruscan art is the figurine of the "Sarcophagus of the Spouses" that dates back to the late sixth-century BCE and is presently on display at the Villa Giulia. Molded from terracotta, the sculpture depicts a married couple reclining together at a banquet in the afterlife and symbolizes a celebration of death and new life in the form of a *mystical* marriage. Jung writes, "In the light of eternity, it is a wedding . . . . The soul attains, as it were, its missing half, it achieves wholeness" (*Memories, Dreams, Reflections* 314).

Many homes in India feature artifacts related to the goddess, Kali, who personifies death in her necklace formed from human skulls. Such an image may be horrifying to those in Western cultures, but for the Hindus, this depiction of Kali as a goddess associated with death reminds individuals that death cannot be avoided, but rather that this dimension of existence must be incorporated into life. Kali represents the illusion of linear time and thus destroys the false consciousness of the ego. For the Hindu, accepting mortality enables the possibility to find freedom in the realm of the gods, and so Kali's frightening personification of death is closely associated with the living.

Elaborate funeral burial rites and rituals carried out by many ancient civilizations also opened a threshold to the *imaginal* world of myth. In *The Rites of Passage*, Arnold van Gennep explains, "During mourning, the living mourners and the deceased constitute a special group, situated between the world of the living and the world of the dead, and how soon living individuals leave that group depends on the closeness of their relationship with the dead person" (147).

The journeys to the otherworld embarked upon by the deceased were aided by certain rites that incorporated the imagined geographical areas that the deceased were traveling to. What is of supreme importance is that the deceased must undertake a journey. As far back as 35,000 to 10,000 years ago, during the Cro-Magnon era, the corpses of the dead were bound and placed in a fetal position, painted with red ochre and decorated with shells. Provisions and icons of the mother goddess were placed around them in order to ensure a safe transition to the otherworld.

Excavations of many ancient burial sites portrayed the mythic belief in death, symbolizing new birth. Carol Zaleski writes, "The ceremonial behavior toward the dead which we see embedded in the earth we excavate is nearly universal in historic times; and whenever one finds burial with grave goods or ritual cremation, sacrificial meals, or prescribed acts of mourning, such practices are but satellites of a much larger system of myths and rites that portray and sustain the cycles of life, death and rebirth" (*Otherworld Journeys* 12).

For the ancient Egyptians, Celts, Etruscans, and Greeks, this *imaginal* voyage was also the reason that the dead were often provided with a replica, or sometimes a real boat with oars and given food, clothing, tools, and other essential items for the passage to the afterlife. The Greeks also provided the deceased with a coin to pay Charon, the ferryman, for the boat ride across the River Styx to the underworld. This symbolic motif of giving money to ensure a safe passage has been found in many other cultures. The Slavs gave monetary offerings to the deceased to pay for the trip to the otherworld, and in the tradition of the Japanese Buddhists, coins were set aside to pay for the ferry expedition across the Sanzu.

Arnold van Gennep's research into funeral and burial rites also unearthed an interesting fact; for it was presumed that rites of separation would be the main feature of such ceremonies, but, instead, rites of transition, practiced to ensure the deceased would be incorporated into the realm of the dead, assumed a greater importance and were more fully elaborated upon (146). The Egyptian rite of the mummification of the corpse of the deceased was in preparation for a dynamic nocturnal resurrection and the myth of the rebirth of Osiris/Ra symbolized the destiny of all those that had led a good life.

The *imaginal* world exists beyond the world of time, space, and logic and provides a mystical experience of *another* dimension of reality.

Chapter Nine

The Power of Story

During medieval times Western culture began to reject the structure of myth. This dissolution of imaginative ways of viewing the world resulted in a loss of connection to the primordial motifs that manifested from a *feminine* universe, which not only personified and preserved a sacred wisdom, but also provided a foundation for religious traditions and understanding the mystery of death. In early cultures, myths of death and the images of the gods were not avoided, but accepted as integral parts of life.

As the maternal universe was disbanded, the feminine influence was edged out of consciousness. Transcendence and a merging with "God" became replaced with a narcissistic view of the world and resulted in nature being stripped of its sacred and spiritual dimensions. Historical changes in the way humans imagine death can be directly linked to the death of connection to the female soul in nature. During the sixteenth and seventeenth-centuries, the Cartesian unimaginative outlook resulted in the loss of experiencing a sense of interconnectedness with the rhythms of the natural world that symbolize the motif of death and rebirth, and primordial images that once instilled a sense of order prevailing in the cosmos.

Religious symbolism expressed certain moral and mental attitudes, inherited from those depicted in ancient resurrection myths that were closely aligned with the natural world. However, as the myth of medieval Christianity died in Europe and became replaced by a form of sterile objectivity, religious dogmas excluded and disassociated from the voice of nature. The French philosopher René Descartes (1596-1650), influenced much of Western thought during this period. In Meditation on First Philosophy, he dismisses the numinous quality of nature as being part of some malign force, whose archetypal energies were divested in deceiving him. He writes, "I shall consider that the heavens, the earth, colors, figures, sound, and all other external things are nought but the illusions and dreams of which this genius has availed himself in order to lay traps for my credibility."

The loss of the image of God had dire consequences and led to the emergence of a tension within the human being that created a state of fear and isolation. The yearning of the psyche to reinvent some form of escape from the gulf of emptiness and reunite with some form of authentic structure became crucially important. With no mythic foundation to support an understanding of death, many look to science and medicine to preserve life at all costs and death is often viewed as the ultimate failure rather than part of the natural life cycle. This approach leaves individuals unable to cope when the inevitability and absoluteness of death enters life; for denial of death and loss of connection to the symbolic metaphors leaves people in a spiritually impoverished wasteland.

The mythological world appeared to be dismissed as the relic of a past era and its symbolism banished to the realms of the unconscious. However, from the moment of birth, it is still the power of *story* that shapes an individual's life. Myths of the ancestors and cultural backgrounds give a person a sense of identity and belonging. Similarly, the quest to find a deeper sense of purpose and meaning can still be accessed through the *imagination*, which reconnects humans to ancient beliefs; for myths of the ancient eternal gods can provide a spiritual compass to rediscover the elusive sense of *home*. In *Living Myths: How Myth Gives Meaning to Human Experience*, J. F. Bierlein writes, "A sacred history, common to all mythic systems, is a record of the numinous past that is both a pattern for the present, and in the worlds of the German philosopher Martin Heidegger (1889-1976), the 'eternal now' that is always there, but only truly real as we encounter it" (3).

Jung suggested that amplification of mythical archetypes was a way to rediscover the image of "God" within the psyche, but in this modern-day world, where can we look to experience the same symbolism and motif of death and rebirth that was at the heart of many ancient myths in order to enrich our own personal myth about death and dying?

Deathbed visions are reported to manifest when a dying person approaches death. Like the archetypal content of ancient myths, these visions suggest the possibility of a realm that exists beyond the one perceived through the five senses. Early pioneers investigating this phenomenon include Dr. James Hyslop, who published the book, *Psychical Research and the Resurrection*, in 1908, and Sir William Barrett, a physics professor at the Royal College of Science in Dublin, who presented his findings in *Deathbed Visions*, published in 1926.

The results of exhaustive contemporary studies carried out on deathbed visions by Karlis Osis and Erlendur Haraldsson were detailed in their book, *At the Hour of Death*, published in 1977. This research, which included the testimony of over one thousand participants from the United States and India, was based on both Western and Eastern cultural mythological backgrounds, which are radically different. Although the study had a rigorous scientific aim, the experiential aspect of the dying process was extremely important. Both Osis and Haraldsson believe that death is not an intellectual problem to be solved, but rather presents a mystery that needs to be understood from the depth of the human being. Therefore, they obtained direct testimony from patients whenever possible. Their research indicates that certain people approaching death experience archetypal visions of a similar nature:

They see apparitions of deceased relatives and friends. They see religious and mythological figures. They see nonearthly environments characterized by light, beauty and intense color. These experiences are transformative. They bring with them serenity, peace, elation, and religious emotions. The patients die a "good death" in strange contrast to the usual gloom and misery commonly expected before expiration. (2)

Osis and Haraldsson's study determined that although religious images manifesting in deathbed visions varied from culture to culture, the nature of the visions contained core mythological components, which included an out-of-body state that culminated in a sensation of passing through darkness into light.

An elevation in the mood of the dying person was also observed, indicating some profound inner change, which was often alarming to medical staff witnessing such an event. It is suggested that during the dying process, a psychic sensitivity may be activated that operates outside normal consciousness of the physical body and personality, which transcends the fear of death and results in feelings of peace and serenity. Such transformation could be viewed as an appropriate response from the dying person to visions or images of a transcendent reality. It has been established that the dying are more likely to experience deathbed visions when fully conscious or alert, rather than when their faculties and abilities to communicate are impaired through the use of medication or a state of delirium. Only a few patients included in the survey were on any form of drug therapy.

An interesting observation was made in relation to the nature of the visions, indicating that although people tend to translate the archetypal imagery into symbolic figures from their own religious belief systems—this was not always the case. Osis and Haraldsson write, "Occasionally it is depicted in terms of the ancient mythology that the patient learned in school. For example, one man saw his wife standing beside a river, waiting for him. It seemed to be the 'River of Forgetfulness' which flows between the two worlds, as related in the Greek myth of Lethe" (41). Although there are similarities in the archetypal patterns of such experiences, this particular example indicated that symbolism or imagery encountered was not always dictated by the religious orientation or mythology of the dying person, but may funnel into a "collective" of stored symbolism depicting an afterlife state. However, core components of such a vision that include feelings of peace, beauty, harmony, and serenity, remained the same for all, regardless of whether the person was Muslim, Christian, Jewish, or Hindu (41).

By far the most compelling testimony from individuals experiencing a deathbed vision is that they view the images of deceased relatives or religious entities as being transition guides. However, if deathbed visions confirm the universality of the myth of the reality, or hope of the afterlife, why don't all people close to dying recall having such an experience? Although the mystery of what takes place in death cannot be fully answered by those who are not dying, but merely witnesses to such an event, it could be that not all dying individuals remember having a deathbed vision. Furthermore, not all these visions occur at the moment of death, but can be experienced sometime before.

Transition guides or *psychopomps* are well known in world mythologies and their role was to ensure a safe transition for the newly deceased soul. They were depicted on funerary art and have often been associated with images from the animal kingdom, including dogs and a variety of birds. For the ancient Greeks it was Hermes, who became the guide to the underworld after making a pact with Hades, in which he agreed to keep a register of the dead and assist souls to their final place of rest. In Roman mythology, it was Mercury, who shared many characteristics with Hermes that acted as the transition guide. In ancient Egypt, the jackal-headed Anubis was the leader of souls. For the Etruscans, Charun, who was depicted with pointed ears and snakes around his arms, and sometimes shown with enormous wings, fulfilled this important role. In Hinduism, the deity known as Agni was known as the intermediary between mortals and the gods. The Islamic Archangel of Death, known as Azrael, collected the souls of the dead. Often in contemporary Western deathbed visions, the guides are Christian religious images that can include Jesus or heavenly angelic beings. In *The Human Encounter with Death*, Stanislav Grof and Joan Halifax write, "Mythological systems have not only detailed descriptions of afterlife realms, but frequently complex cartographies to guide souls on their difficult posthumous journeys" (2).

The archetypal motif of the psychopomp also appears in fairy tale form, and a rendering of the core components of the phenomenon that includes the appearance of a transition guide and heavenly vision shortly before death, can be found in the fairy tale of *The Little Match Girl*. The psychic meaning of the fairy tale is conveyed through symbolic images that can illuminate archetypal patterns of the collective unconscious. Although originally written to illustrate the plight of child labor, Hans Christian Anderson's simple tale contains the central elements found in deathbed visions; for the fairy tale encapsulates recurrent patterns, symbolic of an ancient wisdom.

In the tale, a young girl is out on the freezing streets selling matches on New Year's Eve. Stiff with cold, the child dared to strike a few matches to warm herself and witnessed archetypal symbolism in the form of a great feast, a Christmas tree blazing with lights, and candles that extended into twinkling stars. The girl lit yet another match and the night appeared to transform into day, as her grandmother, looking kind and loving, appeared in the flame's circle. "She lifted the little girl into her arms, and they soared in a halo of light and joy, far, far above the earth, where there was no more cold, no hunger, no pain, for they were with God" (25). The following morning on New Year's Day, the body of the child was found after she had frozen to death on the last night of the year.

The archetypal motifs and numinous content of this story depict death and resurrection portrayed through Christian symbolism and imagery of ascension, together with the metaphor of the ending of the old year and beginning of the new, which was celebrated by many ancient cultures. The appearance of a deceased relative to escort the child to the heavenly realms is one that has many similarities to contemporary deathbed visions. The halo of light is also a motif of a numinous, transpersonal encounter. The archetypes that manifest in this tale appear unadorned and in their purest form, but they reflect spiritual beliefs handed down the generations in an oral tradition.

Even though interest in a mythological world waned, deathbed visions seem to point to the distinct possibility that the primordial images associated with surviving death, which are retained in the collective unconscious, still linger in the human psyche. The ancient message symbolizing transcendence over death repeats itself through the manifestation of archetypal phenomena at the moment of death.

The phenomenon known as a *deathbed vision* can occur when a person close to dying encounters mythological beings and glimpses of an apparent afterlife are clearly seen.

Chapter Ten

Contemporary Otherworldly Journeys

Perhaps the most interesting fact for those interested in myths of an afterlife is how contemporary otherworldly journeys, (known as near-death experiences), like modern-day deathbed visions, share many of the archetypal characteristics and symbolism displayed in resurrection myths and the Books of the Dead from ancient civilizations. In this final chapter of our short voyage through the mythologies depicting an afterlife state, these similarities will be explored in order to illustrate how the motif of death and rebirth still manifests in the experiences of many ordinary individuals, whose lives and beliefs have been transformed and revitalized in their brief glimpses of another realm of consciousness.

A near-death experience is said to occur in certain individuals, who enter the threshold of death and display no visible life signs. These people are termed to be "clinically" dead for a period of time ranging from several minutes up to an hour or longer, but they are later resuscitated and give very similar archetypal accounts of leaving the constraints of the physical body, and then describe passing through a tunnel or void, before being ushered into the most brilliant light. They may be greeted by an entity that most people refer to as "God" or a higher being. Following a life review in which experiencers see a panoramic hologram that presents sequences of their entire past and sometimes future life, feelings of ecstatic unconditional love and bliss are experienced, often accompanied by hearing magnificent music.

Some survivors claim to view the miracle of creation. Many say they are given specific information about the deeper, spiritual aspects of life and express disappointment at having to return to their physical bodies. These central recurring patterns and motifs, which can also include crossing a border, such as a fence or lake of water, define the core components of the NDE, although they may not all occur in each instance and do not specifically follow any sequence.

Near-death survivors find it hard to integrate the magnitude of their experience in a world that is often skeptical about the phenomenon. However, a 1982 Gallup Poll reported that out of the twenty-three million people in the United States, who had a close call with death, eight million described a near-death experience that included some kind of mystical encounter. These contemporary near-death experiences contain similar patterns to those of resurrection myths and ancient otherworldly journeys and have become a source of interest and curiosity. Such narratives may well inspire individuals to learn more about themselves and answer the same existential questions addressed by ancient myths. Many early hero myths portray how the hero transcends death and returns with what Jung describes as being "a more perfect, richer and stronger personality than the ordinary mortal" (*Jung on Death and Immortality* 131).

The growing number of NDEs, reported from all over the globe, may also provide humans with the opportunity to reconnect with the eternal archetypal and symbolic dimensions of death and dying, and thus stimulate the imagination to view the mythology of dying in a more creative way. These near-death narratives are of great interest, because they address the subject of death that is a taboo in many areas of societies both psychologically and culturally. The two contrasting ideas on what death may mean—the total annihilation of consciousness or the widely held mythic belief that death may present the transition of the soul into another dimension—are widely debated topics that affect human behavior. In *Life at Death*, NDE researcher, Dr. Kenneth Rings, reminds us, "What we learn about death may make an important difference in the way we live our lives" (184).

The NDE survivor describes an out-of-body experience and encountering a vision of "God," which results in a conviction of an afterlife state. In ancient Greece, initiates of the ancient Mystery Cults sought to conjure up archetypal images of their supreme deities in order to manifest religious and spiritual symbolism, which signified transcendence over death. Through reenacting these mysterious dramatic myths of transformation from death to rebirth, the continual process of life, and the possibility of immortality was revealed; as the symbolic image of the continual renewal of a vegetation deity represented the archetype of rebirth and an immortal quality that is likened to the cycles of nature.

The initiates participating in the Eleusinian Mystery rites described witnessing the archetype of rebirth reflected in the most brilliant light appearing from a dark cave. Initiation into the great Mystery traditions was believed to be a rehearsal for the dying process, so that at the moment of death, the landscape would appear familiar and initiates would be ready to transition into a new form of existence. This experience of light is also one of the main components of the near-death experience. There are parallels to these ancient rites in the spring three day festival of Easter celebrated in the Christian tradition.

The Eleusinian Mystery cults comprised of a mystical trinity of deities—Persephone, Hades, and Eubouleus, a mysterious figure, who was referred to as being connected to Dionysos, Persephone, and Zeus. The role of Eubouleus in this triad was clearly thought to represent wisdom that would not only perfect the world, but also help individuals to die in a more confident state through living a good life. Persephone's marriage to Hades seemed to personify death, but also hinted that through death, life was enriched by the experience. The myth gave hope for the human condition that was initiated through a beatific vision of the goddess. The archetype of the trinity also appears in

Christianity and in both myths symbolizes the human stages of *being, annihilation, and transformation.* Edward Edinger suggests that this archetype is one that "gives structure and meaning to the dynamic, temporal events of human life" (*Ego and the Archetype* 185).

Initiates of the Eleusinian Mysteries may only have participated in the rites once during their lifetimes. However, such powerful rituals created a sacred portal that Huston Smith believes seemed "regularly to have opened a space in the human psyche for God to enter" (*Cleansing the Doors of Perception* 115). A painted plaque dating back to the fifth-century BCE, which is dedicated to Demeter, depicts a blind man, Eukrates, who even without sight had *seen* the goddess. Similarly, individuals who have an NDE usually only experience such an event once. However, even those who are blind describe *seeing* mystical visions. Elisabeth Kübler-Ross suggests that during NDEs, people experience a sense of wholeness, which includes a restoration of sight in those who have no vision in everyday consciousness (*The Wheel of Life* 190).

The concept of leading a good life in preparation for the after death state was of paramount importance to the ancient Egyptians and they paid homage to Osiris, because they believed in his supernatural abilities as a resurrection deity that they would unite with following death. The near-death survivor describes a life review and the Egyptians believed that following death, a similar review took place in the presence of Osiris. It is also possible to see the similarity of coming forth into the light contained in the myth of Osiris as being an integral part of both contemporary and ancient near-death journeys. The Egyptian myth of Osiris resulted in the deceased becoming "one" with Osiris. The NDE appears to echo this ancient metaphor of alchemical transformation, through symbolizing that consciousness exists beyond the dead body and a meeting with "God."

Plato's myth of Er contains a reminder of the pure light that extended over all of heaven and earth. Er's ascent into the heavenly realms contains a similar sequence and much of the same symbolism found in otherworldly journeys spanning over thousands of years. Kenneth Ring believes that these events unfold in accordance with "a *single pattern*, almost as though the prospect of death serves to release a stored, *common* 'program' of feelings, perceptions, and experiences" (*Life at Death* 15).

Part of the human being's earthly incarnation may involve the need to rediscover the core meaning of such a vision of light, which is also said to manifest during the NDE and is often described as having a golden hue. Although of brilliant intensity, this light does not damage the eyesight of the experiencer and is described as being comforting, restful, and of great beauty. This light would seem to signify emerging from the darkness, and thus symbolize a threshold to a new phase of experience. The appearance of the light during an NDE bears much resemblance to that described in numinous religious experiences and visions. There are also parallels between the archetypal manifestations of the *bardo* states and the near-death journey; for the clear light is apparent in both and near-death survivors bring back the same message contained in the *bardo* and Buddhist teachings—that of realizing the essential qualities in life.

In the one of the earliest accounts of a near-death journey that was narrated by the Venerable Bede, the reluctance to leave the beauty and light of the vision was recorded. Contemporary near-death experiences can also contain the archetypal images and symbolism described in Bede's narration, such as the splendor of the light, the beauty of the paradisiacal vision of an afterlife, a life review, and occasional hellish aspects. The more disturbing visions or difficult challenges to overcome are also depicted in resurrection myths, including Inanna's descent. However, the same unwillingness to return to the physical body was discovered in early research into the NDE carried out by

Elisabeth Kübler-Ross. She interviewed approximately 20,000 individuals from diverse cultures, including Native Americans, Muslims, Protestants, and Eskimos, who all claimed to have had an NDE. Following this exhaustive study, she concluded that such narratives were authentic descriptions of what took place at the moment of death, as consciousness appeared to separate from the body.

The beautiful transcendent melodies of Orpheus would also appear to linger in the collective archetypal realms and still be accessible in the altered state of consciousness taking place during the NDE. Ring relates a near-death survivor describing how she heard the most beautiful "spiritual" music in a very pretty valley (*Life at Death* 62). Veteran NDE researcher, Raymond Moody, also writes of a similar case, "A young woman who nearly died from internal bleeding associated with a blood clotting disorder says that at the moment she collapsed, 'I began to hear music of some sort, a majestic really beautiful sort of music'" (*Life After Life* 30). For the individual said to experience such an altered state, these ancient musical echoes seem to herald a homecoming and glimpse of eternity.

NDE accounts are also consistent with the myth of reincarnation, a central tenet of Eastern religions, such as Hinduism. Although such a diverse difference in beliefs suggest a dualism existing in myths of an afterlife state, in which traditional Western theories view the soul as returning to a spiritual realm and God, as opposed to a continuation of the matter bound life-death cycle of Eastern philosophy, liberation and unification still form the basis and foundation of these varying traditions.

Mythologies of reincarnation suggest that beyond one's personal history and identity, there exists a "collective" identity known to reincarnationists as an *oversoul*, which embodies an expanded form of consciousness, integrating the experiences of personal life. Research suggests near-death experiencers are more open to the myths of reincarnation, because these ideas are more plausible following an NDE.

The image of a living hell in which individuals are punished for living an unjust life is one of the most frightening imaginings to the humans being. There are occasional narratives of NDEs that contain these kinds of disturbing visions; and the mystery of why a negative near-death journey should be experienced is the subject of much debate amongst researchers. The poet William Blake described a vision of hell in *The Marriage of Heaven and Hell*, written during 1789-90. Blake uses "proverbs" from hell to suggest that this realm is not one of punishment, but rather a place that contains repressed Dionysian energy. For Blake, the horrors of hell, and perceiving this disowned shadow Dionysian aspect of the human being, had an alchemical and purifying effect.

The metaphor of the personal becoming involved in the collective reservoir of suffering, which ultimately results in transformation, is portrayed in the myth of the death of Christ, who during his crucifixion, was to suffer the sins of the world and then ascend to the heavenly realms. The myth of Inanna is one that psychologically symbolizes the need to integrate the light and shadow aspects of the psyche. Inanna is required to journey to the underground and meet the terrifying Ereshkigal, who represents her "other" Self. In hero myths, battles and difficulties must also be overcome with such entities as dragons, demons, and serpents, before the hero succeeds in liberating his people from annihilation and death. There are also similarities with the images of wrathful deities that appear in the second bardo state of *Choni Bardo*, but this frightening stage of the journey acts as a purification process. Similar images of hell have been recorded in many world religions, and the Zoroastrian tradition includes an image of dark caverns of hell where sinners huddle in misery. In Christian mythology, St. Paul describes how an evil man loses his soul to a dark angel.

For those believing they have experienced fearful NDEs, the

theory of such negative events representing a "collective" fear of ego-death is an interesting one. This type of NDE with archetypal images of painful suffering does not necessarily reflect that a particular individual has led an unworthy life, but rather that the person has been drawn into a "collective" pool of suffering. Hellish NDEs, like ancient resurrection myths that share similar challenges, may simply incorporate rites of purification. In *Dark Night, Early Dawn*, Christopher M. Bache writes:

> Drawing upon these religious parallels, we might suggest that NDEs also have a wrathful and blissful aspect, a frightening and ecstatic face. The fiery dungeons and taunting demons in hellish void NDEs might be seen as their wrathful form. Though difficult and painful to confront, their intent is simply spiritual purification. Paradoxically, *the severity of our pain in this confrontation is a measure of how much more we are becoming than we have yet managed to be, both individually and collectively.* (123)

Although it would appear that the individual is no longer open to hearing the voice of God on a conscious level, the unconscious still provides a portal for reconnection to a sacred identity. The resurgence of interest in the near-death experience and its archetypal components may offer humans the chance to reevaluate and amplify the meaning of an imagined relationship with God. These narratives, which imply a meeting with the archetype of "God," may help reinstall the belief that this image continues to live within the psyche. Invoking such an apparition or encounter with the gods was the objective in ancient Mystery cults. Rites of deification projected such images as Dionysos and Persephone, resulting in participants believing they had encountered the deities and experienced the feeling of immortality. Religious imagery, such as Christ, manifesting in contemporary NDEs is not that surprising, given the roots of Christianity are steeped in connection to Egyptian mythology and the resurrection of Osiris. The near-death journey is prevalent at the present volatile time in world history. Carol Zaleski suggests, "Although it addresses persistent hopes and fears concerning death, other-worldly narration is a 'wave' phenomenon rather than a constant. It seems to recur when it is needed most, that is, when the way society pictures itself and its surroundings is so changed as to threaten to dislocate the human being" (100).

Certainly, hope appears to be an integral part of human experience and, like ancient resurrection myths and other-worldly journeys—the NDE motif offers a narrative that generates hope.

Can near-death otherworldly narratives and deathbed visions be explained through Corbin's theory of the *mundus imaginalis*? Do these individuals at the moment of death enter the *imaginal* world of myth that is not regulated by time, space, and logic? Corbin writes, "Some of these testimonies cannot be entertained let alone understood except on the condition of having at one's disposal an ontology of the *mundus imaginalis* and a metaphysics of the active Imagination as an organ inherent in the soul and regulated in its own right to the world of subtle corporeity" (*Spiritual Body* xviii).

Jung suggests the importance to the individual of myths, which can dispel the rational fear of death, as being more than a descent into a darkened pit. "Myth, however, can conjure up other images for him, helping and enriching pictures of life in the land of the dead" (*Memories* 306).

The ancient imagining of death being a phase of development is borne out by those having an NDE. During such an archetypal journey, experiencing a sense of "oneness" with everything is experienced. Such a perception of *wholeness* gives rise to feelings of a joyous and a harmonious unity with all of humankind, nature, the universe, and God. In this state of being, the notion of a numinous eternity is fully experienced, regardless of whether the person concerned has any prior religious convictions.

Jung related his own near-death story, following a heart attack in 1944, to a world where many would dispute the validity of such an experience. But according to Jung, "mythic man" demands the need to go beyond the limitations of science and the intellect; for the mysterious myths of the psyche bring healing and speak of inexplicable matters, such as death and immortality, of which the individual has no real knowledge. Through clues from the unconscious manifesting in the archetypal world of mythic stories, there exists the possibility to gain some understanding. Jung argues that if such an idea was presented to him in "mythic" traditions, "I ought to take note of it. I even ought to build up a conception on the basis of such hints, even though it will forever remain a hypothesis which I know cannot be proved" (*Memories* 302). Philosopher Michael Grosso suggests that the NDE represents an archetype—the *archetype of death and enlightenment*, which fits into an archetypal structure and pattern that deals with a specific situation in life—that of physical death. These archetypal energies are not static, but remain fluid as they reveal an abundance of recurring motifs associated with near-death journeys, in which the common thread is transformation ("The Archetype of Death and Enlightenment" 132).

Narratives of near-death experiences, like many myths, may also illustrate how archetypal patterns address human experience and give guidance on the essential key elements of life. This is achieved through clearly defining how the individual is a finite creature that is separated from the numinous sacred, but continually strives to achieve individuation and transcendence, in order to find a spiritual identity in the mysterious realms of the cosmos.

It is also possible that early cultures, such as the Egyptians, had a mythological knowledge of near-death journeys in making their assumptions of an eternal soul. Ancient Egyptian texts describe an experience very similar to contemporary NDEs; and the alchemical metaphor of new life arising from dead matter was one that was depicted in vegetation myths of many ancient civilizations. Alchemical texts from ancient Egypt reflected allegories symbolizing what took place as dead matter in the form of a corpse, transformed into divine spirit. During a core NDE, awareness of the body alters and such a radical shift in consciousness indicates that transformation, similar to that imagined in ancient alchemical metaphors, may well take place during an NDE. The archetypal motif of death and rebirth repeats a recurring message that manifests from the collective psyche; thus indicating that in all probability, ancient civilizations, including the Egyptians, had knowledge of the archetypal symbolism and metaphors contained in near-death journeys, which was incorporated into a mythic structure that was handed down the generations. Contemporary near-death experiences open up a new paradigm for the expression of these ancient archetypal motifs.

Contemporary Near-Death Experiences may well manifest as _living_ myths that continue to reflect the sacred principles of many ancient world religions and mythologies concerning life after death.

Bibliography and Selected References

Abram, David. *The Spell of the Sensuous*. New York: Vintage Books, 1977.

Alighieri, Dante. *The Divine Comedy*. Trans. Allen Mandelbaum. New York: Everyman's Library, 1955.

Anderson, Hans Christian, and Rachael Isadora Turner. *The Little Match Girl*. New York: Putnam, 1990.

Bache, Christopher M. *Dark Night Early Dawn: Steps to a Deep Ecology of Mind*. New York: State of New York P, 2000.

Bede. *A History of the English Church and People*. Trans. Leo Sherley-Price. New York: Dorset Press, 1968.

Bierlein, J. F. *Living Myths: How Myth Gives Meaning to Human Experience*. New York: Ballantine, Wellspring, 1999.

Blake, William. *The Marriage of Heaven and Hell*. New York: Dover, 1994.

Bond, D. Stephenson. *Living Myth: Personal Meaning as a Way of Life*. Boston: Shambhala, 1993.

Campbell, Joseph. *Myths to Live By*. New York: Penguin Compass, 1993.

Corbin, Henry. *Spiritual Body and Celestial Earth*. Princeton, NJ: Princeton UP, 1977.

Doty, William G, *Mythography: The Study of Myth and Rituals*. Tuscaloosa: Alabama, UP, 2000.

Edinger, Edward F. *Anatomy of the Psyche*. Chicago: Open Court, 1991.

Eliade. Mircea. *Myth and Reality*. Trans. Trans. Willard R. Trask. Ed. Ruth Nanda Anshen. New York: Harper and Row, 1963.

Freemantle, Francesca. Introduction. *The Tibetan Book of the Dead*. By Guru Rinpoche According to Karma Lingpa. Trans. Francesca Freemantle and Chögyam Trungpa. Boston: Shambhala, 2000.

Grof, Stanislav. *Books of the Dead: Manuals for Living and Dying*. New York: Thames and Hudson, 1994.

Grof, Stanislav, and Joan Halifax. *The Human Encounter with Death*. New York: E. P. Dutton, 1977.

Grosso, Michael. "The Archetype of Death and Enlightenment." *The Near-Death Experience A Reader*. Eds. Lee W. Bailey and Jenny Yates. New York: Routledge, 1996. 127-43.

Harrison, Robert Pogue. *The Dominion of the Dead*. Chicago: Chicago P. 2003.

Huxley, Aldous. *The Doors of Perception & Heaven and Hell*. New York: HarperPerennial, 1990.

Jung, C. G. "The Archetypes and the Collective Unconscious." Trans. R. F. C. Hull. *The Collected Works of C. G. Jung*. Vol. 9:1. Bollingen Series 20, Princeton, NJ: Princeton UP, 1980.

—-. *Jung on Death and Immortality*. Selected by Jenny Yates. Princeton, NJ: Princeton UP, 1999.

—-. *Memories, Dreams, Reflections.* Ed. A. Jaffe. Trans. R. and C. Winston. New York: Vintage, 1989.

—-. "Psychological Types." Trans. Gerhard Adler, R. F. C. Hull. *The Collected Works of C. G. Jung.* Vol. 6. Bollingen Series 20, Princeton, NJ: Princeton UP, 1971.

Kearney, Michael. *Mortally Wounded: Stories of Soul Pain, Death and Healing.* New York: Simon & Schuster, 1996.

Kübler-Ross, Elisabeth. *The Wheel of Life: A Memoir of Living and Dying.* New York: Touchstone, 1998.

Moody, Raymond. *Life After Life.* New York: Bantam Books, 1988.

Osis, Karlis, and Erlendur Haraldsson. *At the Hour of Death.* New York: Hastings House, 1986.

Plato. *Republic.* Trans. G. M. A. Grube. Indianapolis, IN: Hackett P, 1992.

Ring, Kenneth. *Life at Death.* New York: Coward, McCann & Geoghegan, 1980.

van Gennep, Arnold. *The Rites of Passage.* Trans. Monika B. Vizedom and Gabrielle L. Caffee. Chicago: U of Chicago P, 1960.

Zaleski, Carol. *Otherworld Journeys: Accounts of Near-Death Experiences in Medieval and Modern Times.* New York: Oxford UP, 1987.

Further Recommended Reading

Becoming Osiris: The Ancient Egyptian Death Experience. Ruth Schumann Antelme, and Stephanie Rossini.

The Quest for Paradise: Visions of Heaven and Eternity in the World's Myths and Religions. John Ashton and Tom Whyte.

The Hero with a Thousand Faces. Joseph Campbell.

The Myth of the Eternal Return, or Cosmos and History. Mircea Eliade.

The Politics of Myth. Robert Ellwood.

Ritual Texts for the Afterlife: Orpheus and the Bacchic Gold Tablets. Fritz Graf and Sarah Isles Johnston.

The Ultimate Journey: Consciousness and the Mystery of Death. Stanislav Grof.

The Wisdom of the Serpent: The Myths of Death, Rebirth and Resurrection. Joseph L. Henderson and Maud Oaks.

The Ancient Egyptian Books of the Afterlife. Erik Hornung.

Dionysos: Archetypal Image of Indestructible Life. Carl Kérenyi.

The Ancient Mysteries: A Sourcebook. Marvin Meyer.

Alchemy: An Introduction to the Symbolism and Psychology. Marie-Louise von Franz.

Otherworld Journeys: Accounts of Near-Death Experiences in Medieval and Modern Times. Carol Zaleski.

Practicing Conscious Living and Dying: Stories of the Eternal Continuum of Consciousness. Annamaria Hemingway.

BOOKS

O is a symbol of the world, of oneness and unity. In different cultures it also means the "eye," symbolizing knowledge and insight. We aim to publish books that are accessible, constructive and that challenge accepted opinion, both that of academia and the "moral majority."

Our books are available in all good English language bookstores worldwide. If you don't see the book on the shelves ask the bookstore to order it for you, quoting the ISBN number and title. Alternatively you can order online (all major online retail sites carry our titles) or contact the distributor in the relevant country, listed on the copyright page.

See our website **www.o-books.net** for a full list of over 500 titles, growing by 100 a year.

And tune in to myspiritradio.com for our book review radio show, hosted by June-Elleni Laine, where you can listen to the authors discussing their books.

mySpiritRadio